THE WOMAN IN WHITE

She appears out of nowhere, a woman dressed all in white, standing in the moonlight on the lonely heath. Walter Hartright is at first alarmed, but then sees that she is frightened and confused, and needs his help. He speaks kindly to her, walks with her to show her the right road, and soon she disappears into the night again.

This strange meeting begins a chain of events that bring together Walter, Marian and her half-sister Laura, Sir Percival and his Italian friend Count Fosco in a mystery in which nothing is as it seems. And at the heart of the mystery is the sad, lonely figure of the woman in white – her life, her history, and the secret that she is desperate to reveal before she dies.

It is a story of greed and evil, innocence and betrayal, confused identities and cruel deceptions. And also love – a love that begins with heartbreak and misery, where there seems no way forward, no hope for the future. But love does not die easily; it can survive separation, and despair, and even death itself . . .

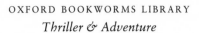

OXFORD BOOKWORMS LIBRARY

Thriller & Adventure

The Woman in White

Stage 6 (2500 headwords)

Series Editor: Jennifer Bassett
Founder Editor: Tricia Hedge
Activities Editors: Jennifer Bassett and Christine Lindop

WILKIE COLLINS

The Woman in White

Retold by
Richard G. Lewis

OXFORD UNIVERSITY PRESS

OXFORD

UNIVERSITY PRESS

Great Clarendon Street, Oxford OX2 6DP

Oxford University Press is a department of the University of Oxford.
It furthers the University's objective of excellence in research, scholarship,
and education by publishing worldwide in

Oxford New York

Auckland Cape Town Dar es Salaam Hong Kong Karachi
Kuala Lumpur Madrid Melbourne Mexico City Nairobi
New Delhi Shanghai Taipei Toronto

With offices in

Argentina Austria Brazil Chile Czech Republic France Greece
Guatemala Hungary Italy Japan Poland Portugal Singapore
South Korea Switzerland Thailand Turkey Ukraine Vietnam

OXFORD and OXFORD ENGLISH are registered trade marks of
Oxford University Press in the UK and in certain other countries

This simplified edition © Oxford University Press 2008

Database right Oxford University Press (maker)

First published in Oxford Bookworms 2002

8 10 9 7

ISBN 978 0 19 479270 7

Printed in China

ACKNOWLEDGEMENTS
Illustrated by: Kanako Damerum and Yuzuru Takasaki

Word count (main text): 31,770 words

For more information on the Oxford Bookworms Library,
visit www.oup.com/bookworms

CONTENTS

PEOPLE IN THIS STORY

Walter Hartright, *a drawing teacher*

Professor Pesca, *a friend of Walter Hartright*

Anne Catherick, *the woman in white*

Mrs Catherick, *Anne's mother*

Mrs Clements, *a friend of Anne Catherick*

Laura Fairlie, *later Laura, Lady Glyde*

Marian Halcombe, *Laura's half-sister*

Frederick Fairlie, *Laura's uncle, owner of Limmeridge House*

Mr Gilmore
Mr Kyrle   } *lawyers to the Fairlie family*

Sir Percival Glyde, *owner of Blackwater Park*

Count Fosco, *an Italian nobleman*

Countess Fosco (Madame Fosco), *the Count's wife, and Laura Fairlie's Aunt Eleanor*

Mrs Michelson, *the housekeeper at Blackwater Park*

Mrs Rubelle, *a nurse employed by Count Fosco*

Mr Dawson, *a doctor*

Fanny, *Lady Glyde's maid*

1

A meeting by moonlight

It was the last day of July. The long hot summer was coming to an end, and I was feeling ill and depressed. I was also short of money, so I had little chance of escaping from the dusty London streets, and would have to spend the autumn economically between my rooms in the city and my mother's house.

My mother and my sister, Sarah, lived in a <u>cottage</u> in Hampstead, in the northern suburbs, and I usually went to see them twice a week. This evening I arrived at the gate of the cottage just as it was starting to get dark. I had hardly rung the bell before the door was opened violently, and my Italian friend, Professor Pesca, rushed out to greet me.

Pesca was a language teacher who had left Italy for political reasons and had made his home in England. He was a strange, excitable little man, who was always trying to be more English than the English. I had met him from time to time when he was teaching in the same houses as I was, and then one day I met him by chance in Brighton. We agreed to go for a swim together in the sea. He was very enthusiastic and it never for a moment occurred to me that he did not know how to swim! Fortunately, when he suddenly sank to the bottom, I was able to dive down and save him. From that day on he was my grateful friend, and that evening he showed his gratitude to me in a way that changed my whole life.

'Now, my good friends,' he said, when we were all in my mother's sitting-room. 'I have some wonderful news for you. I have been asked by my employer to recommend a drawing teacher for a post with a rich family in the north of England. And who do you think I have recommended? The best drawing teacher in the world – Mr Walter Hartright!'

'My dear Pesca! How good you are to Walter!' exclaimed my mother. 'How kind, how generous you are!'

As for myself, although I was certainly grateful for his kindness, I still felt strangely depressed. I thanked him warmly, however, and asked to see the conditions. The note he gave me said that a qualified drawing teacher was wanted by Mr Frederick Fairlie of Limmeridge House, Cumberland, to teach his two young nieces for a period of at least four months. The teacher was to live at Limmeridge House as a gentleman and receive four pounds a week. Letters to show he was of good character would be required.

The position was certainly an attractive one, and I could not understand why I felt so little enthusiasm for it. However, since my mother and sister thought it was a great opportunity, and I had no wish to hurt Pesca's feelings, I agreed to apply for the job.

The next morning I sent my letters of recommendation to the Professor's employer, and four days later I heard that Mr Fairlie accepted my services and requested me to start for Cumberland immediately. I arranged to leave the next day, and in the evening I walked to Hampstead to say goodbye to my mother and Sarah.

When I left them at midnight, a full moon was shining in a dark blue, starless sky, and the air was soft and warm. I decided to take the long route home, and walk across Hampstead Heath before joining the road into the centre of the city. After a while I came to a crossroads and turned onto the London road. I was lost in my own thoughts, wondering about the two young ladies in Cumberland, when suddenly, my heart seemed to stop beating. A hand had touched my shoulder from behind.

I turned at once, my hand tightening on my walking stick.

There, as if it had dropped from the sky, stood the figure of a woman, dressed from head to foot in white clothes. I was too surprised to speak.

'Is that the road into London?' she said.

I looked at her carefully. It was then nearly one o'clock. All I could see in the moonlight was a young colourless face, large sad eyes, and light brown hair. Her manner was quiet and self-controlled. What sort of woman she was, and why she was out so late alone, I could not guess. But there was nothing evil about her – indeed, a kind of sad innocence seemed to come from her.

'Did you hear me?' she said, quietly and rapidly.

'Yes,' I replied, 'that's the road. Please excuse me – I was rather surprised by your sudden appearance.'

'You don't suspect me of doing anything wrong, do you?'

'No, no, seeing you so suddenly gave me a shock, that's all.'

'I heard you coming,' she said, 'and hid behind those trees to see what sort of man you were, before I risked speaking. May I trust you?' Her eyes searched my face, anxiously.

Her loneliness and helplessness were so obvious that I felt great sympathy for her. 'Tell me how I can help you,' I said, 'and if I can, I will.'

'Oh, thank you, thank you. You are very kind.' Her voice trembled a little as she spoke. 'I don't know London at all. Can I get a cab or a carriage at this time of night? Could you show me where to get one, and will you promise not to interfere with me? I have a friend in London who will be glad to receive me. I want nothing else – will you promise?'

She looked nervously up and down the road, then back at me. How could I refuse? Her fear and confusion were painful to see.

'Will you promise?' she repeated.

'Yes.'

We set off together towards the centre of London. It was like a dream – walking along that familiar road, with so strange and so mysterious a companion at my side.

'Tell me how I can help you,' I said, 'and if I can, I will.'

'Do you know any men of the rank of Baronet in London?' she asked suddenly.

There was a note of suspicion in the strange question, and when I said I knew no Baronets, she seemed relieved. I questioned her further, and she murmured that she had been cruelly used by a Baronet she would not name. She told me she came from Hampshire and asked if I lived in London. I explained that I did, but that I was leaving for Cumberland the next day.

'Cumberland!' she repeated softly. 'Ah! I wish I was going there too. I was once happy in Cumberland, in Limmeridge village. I'd like to see Limmeridge House again.'

Limmeridge House! I stopped, amazed.

'What's wrong?' she asked anxiously. 'Did you hear anybody calling after us?'

'No, no. It's just that I heard the name of Limmeridge House very recently. Do you know somebody there?'

'I did once,' she said. 'But Mrs Fairlie is dead; and her husband is dead; and their little girl may be married and gone away . . .'

Perhaps she would have told me more, but just at that moment we saw a cab. I stopped it, and she quickly got in.

'Please,' I said, 'let me see you safely to your friend's house.'

'No, no,' she cried. 'I'm quite safe, and you must let me go. Remember your promise! But thank you – oh! thank you.'

She caught my hand in hers, kissed it, and pushed it away. The cab disappeared into the black shadows on the road – and the woman in white had gone.

Ten minutes later I was still on the same road, thinking uneasily about the whole adventure, when I heard wheels behind me. An open carriage with two men in it passed me, then stopped when they saw a policeman walking further down the street.

'Officer!' cried one of the men. 'Have you seen a woman pass this way? A woman in white clothes?'

'No, sir. Why? What has she done?'

'Done! She has escaped from my asylum.'

An asylum! But the woman had not seemed mad to me. Nervous, and a little strange, perhaps, but not mad. What had I done? Had I helped a woman wrongly imprisoned to escape? Or had I failed to protect a sick person who might come to harm? These disturbing thoughts kept me awake all night after I had got back to my rooms, until at last it was time to leave London and set out for Cumberland.

✿ ✿ ✿

My travelling instructions directed me to Carlisle and then to change trains for Limmeridge. However, because of a long delay I missed my connection and did not get to Limmeridge till past ten. A servant in rather a bad temper was waiting for me at the station with a carriage and when I arrived at Limmeridge House everyone had gone to bed. I was shown to my room and when I at last put out the candle, I thought to myself, 'What shall I see in my dreams tonight? The woman in white? Or the unknown inhabitants of this Cumberland house?'

2

Life at Limmeridge House

When I got up the next morning, I was greeted by bright sunlight and a view of blue sea through the window. The future suddenly seemed full of promise. I found my way down to the breakfast-room and there, looking out of a window with her back turned to me, was a young woman with a perfect figure. But when she turned and walked towards me, I saw to my surprise that her face was ugly. Hair grew on her upper lip, and her mouth was large and firm. It was almost a man's face, but the friendly smile she gave me softened it and made her look more womanly. She welcomed me in a pleasant, educated voice and introduced herself as Marian Halcombe, Miss Fairlie's half-sister.

'My mother was twice married,' she explained, in her easy, friendly manner. 'The first time to Mr Halcombe, my father, and the second time to Mr Fairlie, my half-sister's father. My father was a poor man, and Miss Fairlie's father was a rich man. I've got nothing, and she has a fortune. I'm dark and ugly, and she's fair and pretty.' She said all this quite happily. 'My sister and I are very fond of each other, so you must please both of us, Mr Hartright, or please neither of us.'

She then told me that Miss Fairlie had a headache that morning and was being looked after by Mrs Vesey, an elderly lady who had once been Miss Fairlie's governess.

'So we shall be alone at breakfast, Mr Hartright,' she said. 'As for Mr Fairlie, your employer, you will doubtless meet him later. He is Miss Fairlie's uncle, a single man, who became Miss Fairlie's guardian when her parents died. He suffers from some mysterious illness of the nerves, and never leaves his rooms.'

While we ate breakfast, she described the quiet, regular life that she and her sister led. 'Do you think you will get used to it?' she said. 'Or will you be restless, and wish for some adventure?'

Hearing the word 'adventure' reminded me of my meeting with the woman in white, and her reference to Mrs Fairlie. I told Miss Halcombe all about my adventure, and she showed an eager interest, especially in the mention of her mother.

'But you didn't find out the woman's name?' she said.

'I'm afraid not. Only that she came from Hampshire.'

'Well, I shall spend the morning,' said Miss Halcombe, 'looking through my mother's letters. I'm sure I will find some clues there to explain this mystery. Lunch is at two o'clock, Mr Hartright, and I shall introduce you to my sister then.'

After breakfast Mr Fairlie's personal servant, Louis, came to tell me that Mr Fairlie would like to see me. I followed the servant upstairs and was shown into a large room full of art treasures. There, in an armchair, sat a small, pale, delicate-looking man of about fifty. Despite his fine clothes and the valuable rings on his soft white fingers, there was something very unattractive about him.

'So glad to have you here, Mr Hartright,' he said in a high, complaining voice. 'Please sit down, but don't move the chair. In my state of nerves any movement is painful to me. May I ask if you have found everything satisfactory here at Limmeridge?'

When I began to reply, he at once raised his hand to stop me.

'Please excuse me. But *could* you speak more softly? I simply cannot bear loud voices, or indeed, any kind of loud sound.'

The interview did not last long as Mr Fairlie quickly lost interest in it. He informed me that the ladies would make all the arrangements for their drawing lessons.

'I suffer so much from my nerves, Mr Hartright,' he said. 'Do you mind ringing the bell for Louis? Thank you. *Good* morning!'

With great relief I left the room, and spent the rest of the morning looking forward to lunchtime, when I would be introduced to Miss Fairlie.

✦ ✦ ✦

At two o'clock I entered the dining room and found Miss Halcombe seated at the table with a rather fat lady who smiled all the time. This, I discovered, was Mrs Vesey. We started eating and before long we had finished lunch, with still no sign of Miss Fairlie. Miss Halcombe noticed my frequent glances at the door.

'I understand you, Mr Hartright,' she said. 'You are

wondering about your other student. Well, she has got over her headache, but did not want any lunch. If you will follow me, I think I can find her somewhere in the garden.'

We walked out together along a path through the garden, until we came to a pretty summer-house. Inside I could see a young lady standing near a table, looking out at the view and turning the pages of a little drawing book. This was Miss Laura Fairlie.

How can I describe her? How can I separate this moment from all that has happened since then? In a drawing I later made of her she appears as a light, youthful figure wearing a simple white and blue striped dress and a summer hat. Her hair is light brown, almost gold, and she has eyes that are clear and blue, with a look of truth in them. They give her whole face such a charm that it is difficult to notice each individual feature: the delicate, though not perfectly straight, nose; the sweet, sensitive mouth. The life and beauty of her face lies in her eyes.

Such was my impression, but at the same time I felt there was something about her that I could not explain – something that I ought to remember, but could not. In fact, I was thinking about this so much that I could hardly answer when she greeted me.

Miss Halcombe, believing I was shy, quickly said, 'Look at your perfect student,' and she pointed at the sketches. 'She has already started work before your lessons have begun. You must show them to Mr Hartright, Laura, when we go for a drive.'

Miss Fairlie laughed with bright good humour.

'I hope he will give his true opinion of them and not just say something to please me,' she said.

'May I enquire why you say that?' I asked.

'Because I shall believe all that you tell me,' she answered simply.

In those few words she gave me the key to her own trusting, truthful character.

Later we went for our promised drive, but I must confess that
I was far more interested in Miss Fairlie's conversation than her
sketches. I soon realized I was behaving more like a guest than
a drawing teacher and when I was on my own again I felt uneasy
and dissatisfied with myself.

At dinner that evening these feelings soon disappeared, and
when the meal was over, we went into a large sitting room with
glass doors leading into the garden. Mrs Vesey fell asleep in an
armchair and Miss Halcombe sat near a window to look through
her mother's letters. At my request Miss Fairlie played the piano.

How will I ever forget that peaceful picture? The flowers
outside, the music of Mozart, Miss Halcombe reading the letters
in the half-light, the delicate outline of Miss Fairlie's face against
the dark wall. It was an evening of sights and sounds to
remember for ever.

Later, when Miss Fairlie had finished playing and had
wandered out into the moonlit garden, Miss Halcombe called me.

'Mr Hartright, will you come here for a minute?'

I went over and she showed me a letter.

'It's from my mother to her second husband twelve years ago.
She mentions a lady from Hampshire called Mrs Catherick, who
had come to look after her sick sister living in the village. It seems
she brought her only child with her, a little girl called Anne, who
was about a year older than Laura. I was at a school in Paris at
the time. My mother, who took a great interest in the village
school, says the little girl was slow in learning so she gave her
lessons here at the house. She also gave her some of Laura's white
dresses and white hats, saying she looked better in white than any
other colour. She says that little Anne Catherick was so grateful,
and loved her so much, that one day she kissed her hand and said,
"I'll always wear white as long as I live. It will help me to
remember you."'

Miss Halcombe stopped and looked at me.

'Did the woman you met that night seem young enough to be twenty-two or twenty-three?'

'Yes, Miss Halcombe, as young as that.'

'And was she dressed from head to foot, all in white?'

'All in white.'

From where I sat, I could see Miss Fairlie walking in the garden, and the whiteness of her dress in the moonlight suddenly made my heart beat faster.

'Now listen to what my mother says at the end of the letter,' Miss Halcombe continued. 'It will surprise you. She says that perhaps the real reason for her liking little Anne Catherick so much was that she looked exactly like—'

Before she could finish, I jumped up. Outside stood Miss Fairlie, a white figure alone in the moonlight. And suddenly I realized what it was that I had been unable to remember – it was the extraordinary likeness between Miss Laura Fairlie and the runaway from the asylum, the woman in white.

'You see it!' said Miss Halcombe. 'Just as my mother saw the likeness between them years ago.'

'Yes,' I replied. 'But very unwillingly. To connect that lonely, friendless woman, even by an accidental likeness, to Miss Fairlie disturbs me very much. I don't like to think of it. Please call her in from that horrible moonlight!'

'We won't say anything about this likeness to Laura,' she said. 'It will be a secret between you and me.' Then she called Miss Fairlie in, asking her to play the piano again; and so my first, eventful day at Limmeridge House came to an end.

❖ ❖ ❖

The days passed, the weeks passed, and summer changed into a golden autumn. A peaceful, happy time, but at last, I had to confess to myself my real feelings for Miss Fairlie.

I loved her.

Every day I was near her in that dangerous closeness which exists between teacher and student. Often, as we bent over her sketch-book, our hands and faces almost touched. I breathed the perfume of her hair. I should have put a professional distance between myself and her, as I had always done with my students in the past. But I did not, and it was soon too late.

By the third month of my stay in Cumberland, I was lost in dreams of love and blind to the dangers ahead of me. Then the first warning finally came – from *her*. In the space of one night, she changed towards me. There was a sudden nervous distance, and a kind of sadness, in her attitude. The pain I felt at that moment is beyond description. But I knew then that she had changed because she had suddenly discovered not only my feelings, but her own as well. This change was also reflected in Miss Halcombe, who said nothing unusual to me, but who had developed a new habit of always watching me. This new and awful situation continued for some time until, on a Thursday, near the end of the third month, I was at last rescued by the sensible and courageous Miss Halcombe.

'Have you got a moment for me?' she asked after breakfast. 'Shall we go into the garden?'

We walked to the summer-house and went inside. Miss Halcombe turned to me. 'Mr Hartright, what I have to say to you I can say here. Now, I know that you are a good man who always acts correctly. Your story about that unhappy woman in London proves that. As your friend, I must tell you that I have discovered your feelings for my sister, Laura. Although you have done nothing wrong, except show weakness, I must tell you to leave Limmeridge House before any harm is done. And there is something else I must tell you, which will also give you pain. Will you shake hands with your friend, Marian Halcombe, first?'

She spoke with such kindness that I shook her hand.

'You must leave because Laura Fairlie is to be married.'

The last word went like a bullet to my heart. I turned white, I felt cold. With one word all my hopes disappeared.

'You must put an end to your feelings, here, where you first met her. I will hide nothing from you. She is not marrying for love, but because of a promise she made to her father just before he died. The man she is to marry arrives here next Monday.'

'Let me go today,' I said bitterly. 'The sooner the better.'

'No, not today. That would look strange. Wait till tomorrow, after the post has arrived. Say to Mr Fairlie that you have received bad news and must return to London.'

'I will follow your advice, Miss Halcombe,' I said sadly. 'But may I ask who the gentleman engaged to Miss Fairlie is?'

'A rich man from Hampshire.'

Hampshire! Again a connection with Anne Catherick!

'And his name?' I asked, as calmly as I could.

'Sir Percival Glyde.'

Sir! I remembered Anne Catherick's suspicious question about Baronets, and my voice shook a little as I asked, 'Is he a Baronet?'

She paused for a moment, then answered, 'Yes, a Baronet.'

3

The unsigned letter

As I sat alone in my room later that morning, my thoughts crowded in on me. There was no reason at all for me to connect Sir Percival Glyde with the man who had made Anne Catherick so afraid – but I did. My suffering was great, but even greater was my feeling that some terrible, invisible danger lay ahead of us. Then I heard a knock at my door. It was Miss Halcombe.

'Mr Hartright, I am sorry to disturb you, but you are the only person who can advise me. A letter has just arrived for Miss Fairlie – a horrible, unsigned letter, warning her not to marry Sir Percival Glyde. It has upset my sister very much. Should I try to find out who wrote it or wait to speak to Mr Gilmore, Mr Fairlie's legal adviser, who arrives tomorrow?'

She gave me the letter. There was no greeting, no signature.

Do you believe in dreams, Miss Fairlie? Last night I dreamt I saw you in your white wedding dress in a church, so pretty, so innocent. By your side stood a man with the scar of an old wound on his right hand – a handsome man, but with a black, evil heart; a man who has brought misery to many, and who will bring misery to you. And in my dream I cried for you. Find out the past life of this man, Miss Fairlie, before you marry him. I send you this warning, because your mother was my first, my best, my only friend.

These last words suggested an idea to me, which I was afraid to mention. Was I in danger of losing my balance of mind? Why should everything lead back to the woman in white?

'I think a woman wrote this letter,' said Miss Halcombe. 'It certainly refers to Sir Percival – I remember that scar. What should I do, Mr Hartright? This mystery must be solved. Mr Gilmore is coming to discuss the financial details of Miss Fairlie's marriage, and Sir Percival arrives on Monday to fix the date of the marriage – though Miss Fairlie does not know this yet.'

The date of the marriage! Those words filled me with jealous despair. Perhaps there was some truth in this letter. If I could find the writer, perhaps I would find a way to prove that Sir Percival Glyde was not the honest man he seemed.

'I think we should begin enquiries at once,' I said. 'The longer we delay, the harder it will be to find out anything.'

We questioned the servants and learnt that the letter had been delivered by an elderly woman, who had then disappeared in the direction of the village. People in Limmeridge remembered seeing the woman, but no one could tell us who she was or where she had come from. Finally, I suggested asking the school teacher. As we approached the school door, we could hear the teacher shouting at one of the boys, saying angrily that there were no such things as ghosts. It was an awkward moment, but we went in anyway and asked our question. The teacher could tell us nothing. However, as we turned to leave, Miss Halcombe spoke to the boy standing in the corner:

'Are you the foolish boy who was talking about ghosts?'

'Yes, Miss. But I saw one! I saw it yesterday, in the churchyard. I did! It was – it was the ghost of Mrs Fairlie!'

His answer visibly shocked Miss Halcombe, and the teacher quickly stepped in to explain that the silly boy had said he had seen (or probably imagined) a woman in white standing next to Mrs Fairlie's grave as he passed the churchyard yesterday evening. There was nothing more to it than that.

'What is your opinion of this?' Miss Halcombe asked me as we went out of the school.

'The boy may have seen someone,' I said, 'but not a ghost. I think we should examine the grave. I have this suspicion, Miss Halcombe, that the writer of the letter and the imagined ghost in the churchyard might be the same person.'

She stopped, turned pale, and looked at me. 'What person?'

'Anne Catherick,' I replied. 'The woman in white.'

'I don't know why, but your suspicion frightens me,' she said slowly. 'I will show you the grave, and then I must go back to Laura. We'll meet again at the house later.'

In the churchyard I examined Mrs Fairlie's grave carefully, and noticed that the gravestone had been partly cleaned. Perhaps the person who had done the cleaning would return to finish the job. I decided to come back that evening and watch. Back at the house I explained my plan to Miss Halcombe, who seemed uneasy but made no objection. So, as the sun began to go down, I walked to the churchyard, chose my position, and waited.

After about half an hour I heard footsteps. Then two women passed in front of me and walked to the grave. One wore a long cloak with a hood over her head, hiding her face. Below the cloak a little of her dress was visible – a white dress. The other woman said something to her companion, and then walked away round the corner of the church, leaving the woman in the cloak next to the grave. After looking all around her, she took out a cloth, kissed the white cross and started to clean it.

I approached her slowly and carefully, but when she saw me, she jumped up and looked at me in terror.

There, in front of me, was the face of the woman in white.

'Don't be frightened,' I said. 'Surely you remember me?' Her eyes searched my face. 'I helped you to find the way to London,' I went on. 'Surely you have not forgotten that?'

Her face relaxed as she recognized me, and she sighed in relief. Before this, I had seen her likeness in Miss Fairlie. Now I saw Miss Fairlie's likeness in her. Except that Miss Fairlie's delicate beauty was missing from this tired face, and I could not help thinking that if ever sorrow and suffering fell on Miss Fairlie, then, and only then, they would be the living reflections of one another. It was a horrible thought.

Gently, I began to question her. I told her that I knew she had escaped from an asylum, and that I was glad I had helped her. But had she found her friend in London that night?

'Oh yes. That was Mrs Clements, who is here with me now.

She was our neighbour in Hampshire, and took care of me when I was a little girl. She has always been my friend.'

'Have you no father or mother to take care of you?'

'I never saw my father – I never heard mother speak of him. And I don't get on well with her. I'd rather be with Mrs Clements, who is kind, like you.'

I learnt that she was staying with relations of Mrs Clements at a farm, three miles from the village, but there were other, harder questions I wanted to ask. Who had shut her away in an asylum? Her 'unkind' mother, perhaps? What was her motive in writing the letter to Miss Fairlie, accusing Sir Percival Glyde? Was it revenge? What wrong had Sir Percival done her?

She was easily frightened, easily confused, and could only hold one idea in her mind at a time. I tried not to alarm her. Had she ever, I asked, been wronged by a man and then abandoned? Her innocent, puzzled face told me that was not the answer.

All the time we were talking she was cleaning the gravestone with her cloth.

'Mrs Fairlie was my best friend,' she murmured. 'And her daughter . . .' She looked up at me, then away again, as though hiding her face in guilt. 'Is Miss Fairlie well and happy?' she whispered anxiously.

I decided to try and surprise a confession from her. 'She was not well or happy this morning, after receiving your letter. You wrote it, didn't you? It was wrong to send such a letter.'

Her face went deathly pale. Then she bent down and kissed the gravestone. 'Oh, Mrs Fairlie! Mrs Fairlie! Tell me how to save your daughter. Tell me what to do.'

'You mention no names in the letter, but Miss Fairlie knows that the person you describe is Sir Percival Glyde—'

The moment I said his name she gave such a scream of terror that my blood ran cold. Her face, now full of fear and hatred, told me everything. Without doubt the person who had shut her away in the asylum was Sir Percival Glyde.

At the sound of her scream, Mrs Clements came running and, looking angrily at me, said, 'What is it, my dear? What has this man done to you?'

'Nothing,' the poor girl said. 'He was good to me once. He helped me . . .' She whispered the rest in her friend's ear.

Then Mrs Clements put her arm round Anne Catherick and led her away. I watched them go, feeling great pity for that poor, pale, frightened face.

Half an hour later I was back at the house, and the story I told Miss Halcombe made her very worried.

'I am certain Sir Percival Glyde put Anne Catherick in the asylum,' I said. 'But why? What is the connection between them?'

'We must find out,' said Miss Halcombe. 'We will go to the farm tomorrow, and I will speak to Anne Catherick myself.'

✦ ✦ ✦

The first thing I had to do the next morning was to ask Mr Fairlie if I could leave my job a month early. As his nerves were particularly bad, I could not speak to him directly but had to write a note, explaining that some unexpected news forced me to return to London. In reply I received a most unpleasant letter, informing me that I could go. Once, such a letter would have upset me greatly; now, I no longer cared.

Later Miss Halcombe and I walked to the farm, and Miss Halcombe went in while I waited nearby. To my surprise, she returned after only a few minutes.

'Does Anne Catherick refuse to see you?' I asked.

'Anne Catherick has gone,' replied Miss Halcombe. 'She left this morning, with Mrs Clements. The farmer's wife, Mrs Todd, has no idea why they left or where they went. She just said that Anne Catherick had been disturbed after reading something in the local newspaper a couple of days ago. I looked at the paper and saw that it mentioned Laura's future wedding. Then Mrs Todd said that Anne Catherick fainted last night, apparently in shock at something mentioned by one of the servant girls from our house, who was visiting the farm on her evening off.'

We hurried back to the house to question the servant girl. Miss Halcombe asked her if she had mentioned Sir Percival Glyde's name while at the farm. 'Oh yes,' the girl replied. 'I said he was coming on Monday.'

At that moment a cab arrived and Mr Gilmore, the family friend and legal adviser, got out. He was an elderly man, pleasant-looking and neatly dressed. Miss Halcombe introduced me, and then went away to discuss family matters with him. I wandered out into the garden. My time at Limmeridge House was nearly at an end, and I wanted to say a last goodbye to the places where I had so often walked with Miss Fairlie, in the dream-time of my happiness and my love. But the autumn day was grey and damp, and those golden memories were already fading.

As I returned to the house, I met Mr Gilmore.

'Ah, Mr Hartright,' he said. 'Miss Halcombe has told me how helpful you have been about this strange letter received by Miss Fairlie. I want you to know that the investigation is now in my safe hands. I have written to Sir Percival Glyde's lawyer in London and I'm sure we will receive a satisfactory explanation.'

'I'm afraid I am not so sure as you,' was my reply.

'Well, well,' said Mr Gilmore. 'We will wait for events.'

At dinner that evening – my last dinner at Limmeridge House – it was a hard battle to keep my self-control. I saw that it was not easy for Miss Fairlie, either. She gave me her hand as she had done in happier days, but her fingers trembled and her face was pale. Mr Gilmore kept the conversation going, and afterwards

*In the garden, where I had so often walked with Miss Fairlie,
in the dream-time of my happiness and my love.*

we went into the sitting room as usual. Miss Fairlie sat at the piano.

'Shall I play some of those pieces by Mozart that you like? Will you sit in your old chair near me?' she asked nervously.

'As it is my last night, I will,' I answered.

'I am very sorry you are going,' she said, almost in a whisper.

'I shall remember those kind words, Miss Fairlie, long after tomorrow has gone,' I replied.

'Don't speak about tomorrow.'

Then she played, and at last it was time to say goodnight.

The next morning I found Miss Halcombe and Miss Fairlie waiting for me downstairs. When I began to speak, Miss Fairlie turned and hurried from the room. I tried to control my voice, but could only say, 'Will you write to me, Miss Halcombe?'

She took both my hands in hers, and her face grew beautiful with the force of her generosity and pity. 'Of course I will, Walter. Goodbye – and God bless you!'

She left, and a few seconds later Miss Fairlie returned, holding something. It was her own sketch of the summer-house where we had first met. With tears in her eyes, she offered it to me, 'to remind you', she whispered. My own tears fell as I kissed her hand, then I turned to go. She sank into a chair, her head dropped on her arms. At that moment I knew that Laura Fairlie loved me too. But it was over. We were separated.

4

Arrangements for a marriage

It was a sad day when Walter Hartright left us. Laura stayed in her room all day, and I felt sad and depressed. Poor Mr Gilmore must have had a dull time, and the next morning, when Laura reappeared looking pale and ill, I thought he seemed rather anxious about her. I was anxious too. Laura is such a sensitive and loving person that it was no surprise to me to find that she had grown fond of Walter. Indeed, I have grown fond of him myself. But I honestly believe that time will cure Laura of these feelings.

Two days after Walter left, Sir Percival Glyde arrived. He is forty-five years old but seems younger. He is handsome, and only a little bald, has perfect manners, and is pleasant, agreeable, and respectful. I really must try to like him.

In the afternoon, while Laura was out of the room, Sir Percival referred to Anne Catherick's letter.

'I read Mr Gilmore's letter to my lawyer,' he said, 'and I want to give you a full explanation. Mrs Catherick, you see, worked for me and my family for many years. Her marriage was unfortunate, in that her husband deserted her, and her only child, a girl, became mentally ill and needed to be put in an asylum. So, in recognition of Mrs Catherick's services, I agreed to pay the expenses of a private asylum for the girl. Unfortunately, the girl discovered this and consequently developed a hatred for me. She recently escaped from the asylum and I'm sure she wrote this letter because of her hatred for me. It's all very sad.'

Mr Gilmore found this explanation perfectly satisfactory, and said so. He then looked at me for agreement, but I was struggling with a sense of unease that I could not explain, and hesitated before answering. Sir Percival noticed this at once.

'May I beg you, Miss Halcombe,' he said politely, 'to write to Mrs Catherick to ask if these facts are true?'

I did not want to agree to this, but how could I refuse, without making the situation even more embarrassing than it already was? So I went to the desk, wrote a note, and gave it to him. Without looking at it, he put it in an envelope and wrote the address.

'Now that is done,' he said, 'may I ask if Anne Catherick spoke to Miss Fairlie, or to you?'

'No. She spoke to nobody except Mr Hartright,' I replied.

'Ah, yes, the drawing teacher,' he said thoughtfully. 'And did you discover where Anne Catherick was staying?'

I described the farm to him.

'It is my duty to try to find her,' he continued. 'Tomorrow I will go to this farm and make enquiries.' Soon afterwards he left to go up to his room.

✤ ✤ ✤

That evening and the next day Sir Percival took every opportunity to bring Laura into the conversation, but she hardly took any notice. He went to the farm to make his enquiries about Anne Catherick, but learnt nothing. Then on Wednesday a letter came from Mrs Catherick – a short, business-like letter, thanking me for my note and saying that everything Sir Percival had told me was completely correct.

Why did I still have doubts? This, surely, was enough proof for anyone, but how I wished that Walter Hartright had been there to give his opinion! At Sir Percival's request I now had to give Laura his explanation of Anne Catherick's letter. She listened quietly and showed no emotion, but I noticed that on the table near her hand was the little book of Hartright's drawings. I also had to tell her that the reason for Sir Percival's visit was to fix the day of their marriage.

'I'm afraid he will ask you to decide quite soon, Laura.'

'Oh no, Marian! I can't do that!' she said. 'Please ask him, *beg* him, to allow me more time. I promise to give him a final answer before the end of the year, but not yet, please, not yet.'

Sir Percival agreed to this request, and when Mr Gilmore heard about it, he arranged to have a private talk with Laura.

'I have to return to London tomorrow,' he said to me, 'and I need to discuss the financial side of this marriage with Miss Fairlie before I go. As you know, she will inherit a great deal of money and property when she becomes twenty-one next March, and I must include all this in the marriage agreement in a way that reflects Miss Fairlie's own wishes, and is also acceptable to Sir Percival.'

He had the meeting with Laura the next morning, and in the afternoon he left for London, looking rather sad and thoughtful. Wondering what had been said, I hurried up to Laura's room.

'Oh, Marian, come in,' she said. 'I need to talk to you.'

'What is it, Laura? Is it about the marriage agreement?'

'No. I couldn't even bear to discuss that with Mr Gilmore. I'm ashamed to say that all I could do was cry. He was very kind and good, Marian, and he said that he would look after everything for me. No, what I wanted to tell you was this. I cannot bear the situation any longer. I must end it.'

Her eyes were bright and she spoke with great energy. I began to feel alarmed. 'What do you wish to do, Laura darling? Do you want to be released from your promise to marry Sir Percival?'

'No,' she said simply. 'I cannot break my promise to my father. But I want to tell the truth, and I will confess to Sir Percival that I love someone else.'

'Laura! He has no right to know that!' I said in amazement.

'I cannot deceive him,' she said. 'I have thought it over carefully. After I have told him, let him do as he wishes.'

I looked into her innocent, loving eyes and could say nothing. I just put my arms around her, trying not to cry myself.

'May I speak to him tomorrow, in your presence, Marian?'

I held her tight and agreed – though I was not sure I was doing the right thing. Indeed, I was not sure of anything. I could not understand how I had failed to see how deeply she loved Walter Hartright. For the first time in my life I had made a mistake about her. Now I realized that she would love him all her life.

✤ ✤ ✤

The first thing that happened the next morning did nothing to make me feel more cheerful. A letter arrived for me from poor Walter Hartright. He had decided to leave England and asked me if I could help him find employment abroad. I was then alarmed to read that since his return to London he had neither seen nor heard anything of Anne Catherick, but suspected he had been watched and followed by strange men. I was worried about his state of mind, so I immediately wrote to some friends in London to ask if they could help him find a suitable job in another country. Laura, of course, knew nothing about these letters.

Sir Percival did not join us for breakfast, but sent a message, saying he would meet us at eleven o'clock, as arranged. Laura seemed calm and unusually self-controlled. I had never seen her like this. It was almost as if love had created a new force in her character.

At exactly eleven Sir Percival knocked and entered, with

anxiety and worry in every line of his face. This meeting would decide his future life, and he obviously knew it.

'You may wonder, Sir Percival,' said Laura calmly, 'if I am going to ask to be released from my promise to marry you. I am not going to ask this. I respect my father's wishes too much.'

His face relaxed a little, but I saw one of his feet nervously beating the carpet.

'No, if we are going to withdraw from our planned marriage, it will be because of your wish, Sir Percival, not mine.'

'Mine?' he said in great surprise. 'What reason could I have for withdrawing?'

'A reason that is very hard to tell you,' she answered. 'There is a change in me.'

His face went so pale that even his lips lost their colour. He turned his head to one side.

'What change?' he asked, trying to hide his nervousness.

'When the promise was made two years ago,' she said, 'my love did not belong to anyone. Will you forgive me, Sir Percival, if I tell you that it now belongs to another person?'

Her tears started to fall, and Sir Percival hid his face behind his hand, so that it was impossible to know what he was thinking. He made no answer, and my temper got the better of me.

'Sir Percival!' I said sharply. 'Have you nothing to say? You have already heard more than you have a right to hear.'

'But I didn't ask for that right,' he said, avoiding my question.

'I wish you to understand,' Laura continued, 'that I will never see this person again, and that if you leave me, you only allow me to remain a single woman for the rest of my life. All I ask is that you forgive me and keep my secret.'

'I will do both those things,' he said. Then he looked at Laura, as if he was waiting to hear more.

'I think I have said enough to give you reason to withdraw from our marriage,' she added quietly.

'No. You have said enough to make it the dearest wish of my life to marry you,' he said, getting up and advancing towards her.

Laura gave a cry of surprise, but I had more than half expected this. Every word she had spoken had shown her honesty and her innocence, but these fine qualities had destroyed her own hopes of a release. Sir Percival understood very well the priceless value of a pure and true woman. Why would he give her up now?

'I will do everything I can to earn your love,' he said, 'and perhaps in time I will win it.'

'Never!' she answered, looking more beautiful than ever. 'I will be your true and loyal wife, but never your loving wife.'

'That is enough for me. I accept your loyalty and your truth,' he said, then raised her hand to his lips and silently left the room.

Laura sat without moving. I put my arm around her. At last she said, 'I must resign myself, Marian. If you write to Walter, don't tell him how unhappy I am. And if I die first, please say to him, say what I could never say myself – say I loved him!'

Then she threw herself on the sofa and cried as if her heart was breaking, until at last she fell asleep.

✦ ✦ ✦

In the days that followed it seemed that nothing could prevent this miserable marriage from taking place. I tried to make Laura change her mind, but she was determined to keep her promise, and to do her duty. Mr Fairlie was, of course, very happy that the 'family worry' was now at an end and suggested that the sooner his niece got married the better. This made me very angry, but when I told Laura, I was surprised by her calm reply.

'My uncle is right. I have caused trouble and anxiety to everyone. Let Sir Percival decide on the day for our marriage.'

Sir Percival was delighted by this news, and he then left to prepare for the bride's reception at his house in Hampshire.

I thought that a change would do Laura good, so I arranged for us both to go and stay with some friends in Yorkshire. She passively agreed with my idea. I also wrote to Mr Gilmore, telling him this marriage would now take place.

The next day I received a letter from Walter Hartright, saying that my friends had got him a job on an expedition to Central America. He was going to be the artist for the expedition. He was leaving on 21st November and would be away for six months. I could only hope that this was for the best.

Laura and I then departed for Yorkshire but after only nine days there we received a letter from Mr Fairlie, calling us back to Limmeridge immediately. What could this mean, I wondered?

I found out as soon as we arrived. Mr Fairlie and Sir Percival had agreed on 22nd December for the wedding, provided that Laura also agreed. Would I please persuade her, said Mr Fairlie. His nerves were much too bad to talk to her himself.

I also found our old friend Mr Gilmore, who had come to talk to Mr Fairlie about the marriage agreement. He was leaving that day, and was anxious to speak to me alone before he left.

'I am not at all happy about the financial arrangements in the agreement, Miss Halcombe,' he said, 'but there is nothing I can do about it. I know how fond you are of your sister and I think you ought to know why I am concerned.

'As you will know,' he went on, 'there are three parts to Miss Fairlie's inheritance. Firstly, on Mr Fairlie's death, she will inherit the Limmeridge property and land, and the income from it. If she dies childless, this property will go to a cousin, but the income from it will go to her husband during his lifetime. If she has a son, everything – property and income – will go to the son. No problems there.

'Secondly, when Miss Fairlie reaches the age of twenty-one

next March, she will receive the income from £10,000. This £10,000 will go to her aunt Eleanor, if Miss Fairlie dies before her aunt – which is not very likely. The reason Miss Fairlie's father did not leave the £10,000 to his sister Eleanor on his death was that he disapproved strongly of her marriage to a foreigner, even though the man was an Italian nobleman, Count Fosco.'

'Yes, Laura has told me about that,' I said.

'Well,' Mr Gilmore went on, 'there are no problems there either. But the third part of Miss Fairlie's inheritance is more difficult. Next March she will also inherit £20,000, which will be her own money completely. If she dies before her husband, the income from the £20,000 will go to Sir Percival for his lifetime, and the capital will go to their children. If there are no children to inherit the capital, Miss Fairlie can choose relations and friends to inherit the money when she dies. That's what I proposed, but Sir Percival's lawyer did not accept it. He insists that if Sir Percival survives his wife and there are no children, Sir Percival should receive the capital. In that case, nothing will go to any other member of the family, including you, Miss Halcombe.'

Mr Gilmore sighed deeply. 'I protested strongly. I tried every argument I could, but nothing would change the lawyer's mind. I've discovered, you see, that Sir Percival is always in debt and always in need of cash. My last effort has been to come here, to try and persuade Mr Fairlie to oppose this demand from Sir Percival's lawyer. I am sorry to say I have not succeeded. Mr Fairlie wishes to avoid all responsibility for his niece's marriage arrangements. He says that his niece will not die before Sir Percival anyway, so what is there to worry about?'

Mr Gilmore stood up to go and picked up his hat. 'I shall complete the agreement and send it in. I have no choice. If I don't do it, Mr Fairlie will find another lawyer who will. But I tell you,

Miss Halcombe, no daughter of mine should be married to any man alive under such an agreement as I am forced to make for Miss Fairlie.'

With that, he shook my hand, and without another word he went away to catch his train back to London.

After he had gone, I tried to be sensible. Mr Fairlie was Laura's guardian and if he chose to accept this agreement, there was nothing I could do about it. It was just one more worry about this dreadful marriage. A more immediate worry was the date of the wedding. When I told Laura, she turned pale and trembled.

'Not so soon!' she cried. 'Oh, Marian, not so soon!'

'Well, let me speak to Mr Fairlie, then,' I said, ready to fight for her. 'I will try to change it.'

'No,' she said faintly. 'Too late, Marian, too late! It will only make more trouble. Please tell my uncle I agree.'

I think I would have cried if I had not been so angry. I rushed into Mr Fairlie's room and shouted loudly, 'Laura agrees to the twenty-second' – and rushed out again, banging the door noisily. I hoped I had destroyed his nerves for the whole day.

✦ ✦ ✦

After this the wedding preparations began. The dressmakers came and went all the time; there was packing, and planning, and all kinds of arrangements to make. We heard every day from Sir Percival. After the wedding he proposed to take Laura to Italy for six months. They would meet a number of Sir Percival's friends there, including his best and oldest friend, Count Fosco, whose wife, of course, was Laura's Aunt Eleanor. At least this marriage would bring Laura and her aunt together again, I thought. The Count himself sounded a most interesting person, and I rather hoped that I would meet him one day.

All too quickly the days passed. Sir Percival arrived, looking a little tired and anxious but talking and laughing like the

'Not so soon!' Laura cried. 'Oh, Marian, not so soon!'

happiest of men. The evening after he arrived he went off to the village to ask if anyone had any news of Anne Catherick. No one had heard anything, but I had to admit that it was good of him to continue to try to help her. I have decided to try and think better of him. After all, what reason do I have to distrust him? I am sure that I could like him if I really tried.

It is getting quite easy to like him. Today I spoke to him about the dearest wish of both Laura and myself – that I should be able to live with Laura after her marriage, just as I had always lived with her before. He agreed instantly and seemed delighted with the plan. I would be the ideal, the perfect companion for his wife, he said. Yes, I am beginning to like Sir Percival very much.

❖ ❖ ❖

I hate Sir Percival! He has no sensitivity, no kindness, no good feeling. Last night he whispered something in Laura's ear – she has refused to tell me what it was – and her face turned white with misery. He took no notice at all, and all my suspicions of him have returned. Is he now showing his true character? He seems more restless and nervous than before, and is often sharp and bad-tempered. I have this strange idea that something might happen to prevent the marriage – and that *he* is afraid of that. A foolish thought. I must forget it.

As the day of our separation grows nearer, Laura cannot bear to have me out of her sight. I must be brave and cheerful, for her sake, but my fear will not go away. Will this marriage be the one terrible mistake of her life, and the one hopeless sorrow of mine?

❖ ❖ ❖

It is the twenty-second. No more time for tears. Laura is dressed, and we leave for the church. By eleven o'clock they are married. By three o'clock they are gone. I am blind with crying and can write no more . . .

5

A document for signature

Six long, lonely months passed, and I had little to do but think of absent friends. I received a cheerful letter from Walter Hartright after he arrived in Honduras, and just before he set off with the expedition into the forest. Since then, I have heard nothing. There was no news of Anne Catherick or Mrs Clements. Poor Mr Gilmore fell very ill and had to give up work, but his business is continued by his partner, Mr Kyrle. Mrs Vesey has moved to London to live with her sister, and Mr Fairlie, I believe, is secretly delighted to have his house free of women.

Most of all, of course, I thought about Laura. Many letters came from her, but she said very little in them. She told me she was well, but hardly mentioned her husband, and wrote not a word about Count Fosco, whom they had met in Austria, not Italy. I understood from her silence that she did not like him. All she said was that her Aunt Eleanor, Madame Fosco, was quieter and more sensible than she had used to be.

✢ ✢ ✢

On 11th June I arrived at Blackwater Park, Sir Percival's family home in Hampshire. The waiting was nearly over, and how happy I was! The next day Laura and her husband would return home, together with Count Fosco and his wife, who were going to spend the summer at Blackwater.

In the morning the housekeeper, Mrs Michelson, showed me round the house. It is very old, and much of it is dusty and unused; only one part of the enormous building is comfortable enough to live in.

Later I explored the gardens and the park. The gardens are small and not well kept, and there are so many trees that the house feels shut in by them. I found a path through the trees, which after half a mile brought me to a lake. It was a damp, lonely place. The still dark waters of the lake and the long shadows from the tall trees gave it a gloomy air. Near the lake there was an old boat-house with some seats in it, so I went in and sat down for a rest.

I am not a nervous person generally but when I heard the sound of quick breathing under my seat, I jumped to my feet in alarm. In fact, it was a dog – a small black and white dog, with a bullet wound in its side. I carried the poor creature back to the house and sent for Mrs Michelson to help me.

When she came in and saw the dog lying on the floor, she cried out at once, 'Oh! That must be Mrs Catherick's dog!'

'Whose?' I asked, amazed.

'Mrs Catherick's. Do you know her? She came here to ask for news of her daughter.'

'When?'

'Yesterday. She'd heard that her daughter Anne had been seen in the neighbourhood. But no one knew anything. I suppose the dog ran away into the woods and got shot by the park-keeper.'

I tried to make my voice sound politely interested. 'I suppose you've known Mrs Catherick for some years?'

'Oh no, Miss Halcombe, I never saw her before. She lives at Welmingham, twenty-five miles away. I had heard of her, because of Sir Percival paying for her daughter to go to an asylum. But yesterday, Mrs Catherick asked me not to mention her visit to Sir Percival. That was an odd thing to say, wasn't it, Miss?'

Odd, indeed! But then we had to turn our attention to the poor dog, which, despite our efforts, died a little while later. It was a sad thing to happen on my first day at Blackwater.

✧ ✧ ✧

Later that evening the travellers returned. After my first happiness at meeting Laura, I felt there was a strangeness between us and I realized she had changed. I was sure we would soon get back to normal, but she had lost her innocent openness. She was unwilling to talk about her married life, and I saw that there were no warm feelings between her husband and her. It wasn't long before she asked me about Walter – 'Have you heard from him? Is he well and happy?' – and it was clear to me that she loved him as deeply as ever.

As for Sir Percival, his manners are sharper and less pleasant. On meeting me he simply said, 'Hello, Miss Halcombe. Glad to see you again,' – and then walked past me. Little things seem to annoy him a great deal. For example, the housekeeper told him a man had called to speak to him a week ago but had left no name. Sir Percival demanded a description of the man, which poor Mrs Michelson was unable to give, and Sir Percival stormed out of the room in great anger.

Laura was certainly right about Madame Fosco. Never have I seen such a change in a woman. As Eleanor Fairlie (aged thirty-seven), she wore bright clothes, was silly and foolish, and always talked nonsense. As Madame Fosco (aged forty-three), she wears only grey or black, and sits for hours in silence, doing needlework, rolling up cigarettes for the Count, or just looking at him with the eyes of a loyal dog.

And the man who has achieved this extraordinary change, the man who has tamed this wild Englishwoman? Yes, what can I say about the Count? He looks like a man who could tame anything. If he had married *me*, I would have made his cigarettes, as his wife does. I would have held my tongue when he looked at me, as she holds hers.

How can I explain the power, the attraction, the force that comes from this man? There are many unlikeable or unattractive things about him. For example, he is enormously fat; he seems to have false hair; he is at least sixty years old. He is lazy, jumps at the slightest sudden sound, and has a peculiar fondness for pet animals. He has brought with him a variety of birds and a whole family of white mice, which he often kisses and calls loving names, just as a child might do.

And yet, and yet . . . He is fat, but moves lightly and easily, like a dancer. There is a calmness and a strength about his smooth, unlined face, and his voice is persuasive, gentle, hard to resist. His knowledge of the English language is perfect and he is a well-known expert in chemical science. He speaks in baby language to his white mice, but he talks with intelligence and charm about books in every language, and brings to his conversation experience of life in half the capitals of Europe.

But it is his eyes that I shall always remember – his cold, clear, beautiful grey eyes, eyes which held such a frightening power that I shiver even now to think of it.

I could discover very little about his past from Sir Percival. I only learnt that he had not been to Italy for years; I wondered if this was for political reasons. It seemed he had saved Sir Percival from great danger in Rome once and they had been the closest of friends ever since. It was quite clear that Sir Percival was always anxious to please him and would never go against his wishes.

I wonder whether I am afraid of him too. I certainly never saw a man I would be more sorry to have as an enemy.

❖ ❖ ❖

At lunchtime, a few days after they all returned, a man called Mr Merriman arrived, asking to see Sir Percival urgently. Sir Percival had clearly not expected the visit and looked both alarmed and angry as he left the table.

Neither Laura nor I had any idea who Mr Merriman was, but the Count told us he was Sir Percival's lawyer. I wondered what had happened, as a lawyer does not usually travel from London to Hampshire unless sent for. Mr Merriman must be the bringer of important news – either good or bad.

Count Fosco obviously read my thoughts and said softly to me, 'Yes, Miss Halcombe, something *has* happened.'

Later in the day I was coming from my room when I saw Sir Percival and his lawyer crossing the hall downstairs. They spoke quietly, but clearly enough for their words to reach my ears.

'Yes, Sir Percival,' I heard the lawyer say, 'it all depends on Lady Glyde.'

I immediately stopped when I heard Laura's name and, although I knew it was wrong, continued to listen.

'You understand, Sir Percival, Lady Glyde must sign her name in the presence of two witnesses. If this is done in a week's time, everything will be all right. If not, I may be able to get them to accept a document promising payment in three months. But how that money is to be obtained by then . . .'

They went into the library and I heard no more, but it seemed that Sir Percival had a serious debt and that the solution to it depended on Laura. I immediately went to tell Laura what I had heard. She did not seem surprised.

'I was afraid of something like this,' she said, 'when I heard about that strange gentleman who called, without leaving his name. He had probably come to ask for his money. But don't worry, Marian. I won't sign anything that I might later regret.'

In the evening Sir Percival was unusually polite and pleasant to all of us. What did this mean? I thought I could guess – I was afraid Laura could guess – and I was sure Count Fosco knew. I saw Sir Percival looking at him for approval more than once during the evening. The Count was certainly aware of Sir Percival's financial problems.

The next morning Sir Percival asked Count Fosco, Laura, and myself if we would go to the library for a minute after lunch for a small business matter. Before lunch, however, we all went for a walk to the lake, stopping at the boat-house for a rest.

'Some people call the lake pretty,' said Sir Percival, pointing to the view. 'I call it ugly. It looks just the place for a murder, doesn't it? What do you think, Fosco?'

'My dear Percival,' the Count protested, 'the water is too shallow to hide a body. Only a fool would murder someone here. A wise man would choose somewhere else.'

'Wise men do not murder,' said Laura, looking at him with

dislike. 'I am sure you cannot give me an example of a wise man who has been a criminal.'

'My dear lady,' said the Count, 'it is impossible to give an example, because a wise man's crime is never found out.'

As he spoke, he was playing with his white mice in their little cage, and suddenly noticed that one of them was missing. A few seconds later he found the little animal under a seat, but also found something which seemed to shock him.

'Percival,' he said, 'come here. Look at this in the sand. Blood!'

Everyone seemed alarmed, so I had to explain about the wounded dog I had found.

'Whose dog was it?' asked Sir Percival.

'The housekeeper said it was Mrs Catherick's dog,' I replied, remembering too late that the visit was meant to be kept secret.

'What the devil was Mrs Catherick doing here?'

This question came with such rudeness and anger that I turned away. Count Fosco laid his hand on Sir Percival's arm.

'My dear Percival! Gently, gently!'

To my great surprise, Sir Percival apologized to me, and Count Fosco then said, 'Why not question the housekeeper, Percival, since she seems to know all about it?'

Sir Percival took the point, and immediately left us to return to the house.

The Count seemed fascinated by Mrs Catherick and wanted to know all about her visit. I tried to say as little as possible, but Laura asked questions too, and in the end the Count knew as much as we did about Mrs Catherick and her daughter Anne. I was quite sure, from his surprise at the story, that the Count had known nothing of Anne Catherick, and uneasily I wondered why Sir Percival had not told his closest friend.

When we went back to the house, Sir Percival came to greet

us. 'I am sorry to say I have to leave you. I have to drive a long way and won't be back until tomorrow. First, though, I would like to finish that little business matter. Will you come into the library? It won't take a minute.'

In the library he got a document out of a cupboard and put it on the table. It was folded in such a way that all the writing was hidden and only the places to sign were visible.

Handing a pen to Laura, he said, 'Sign there. You and Fosco are to sign afterwards, Miss Halcombe.'

'What do you want me to sign?' Laura asked quietly.

'I have no time to explain. I have to leave. It's just business,' he said angrily. 'Women don't understand business. Just sign it.'

'But surely I ought to know what I am signing.'

'I see. So you're saying you don't trust me! Is that it? What kind of a wife is that?'

To help Laura, I said, 'I am afraid I cannot be a witness if she doesn't understand what she is signing.'

Sir Percival turned to me furiously. 'How dare you! You're a guest in my house and you take my wife's side against me!'

'Control your unfortunate temper, Percival,' said the Count, and I heard him whisper to him, 'You idiot!'

But Laura had put the pen down and moved to my side.

'Lady Glyde is right,' the Count then said. 'Let the signature wait until tomorrow.'

Sir Percival swore at him, but moved away from the table.

'All right, then,' he said, 'until tomorrow. Anyway, I have to go. But you will sign tomorrow or—' He gave his wife a cold, hard stare, then went out.

As Laura and I moved to the door, the Count approached us. 'You have just seen Sir Percival at his worst,' he said. 'As his old friend, I apologize for him and promise he won't behave like that tomorrow.'

I had begun to realize that I could not hope to remain at Blackwater Park now without the influence and support of the Count, so I answered by thanking him warmly. Then I led Laura out and took her up to my room for a rest.

While we were there, she told me how cruel Sir Percival had been to her since their marriage and how unhappy she was. I tried

'It's just business,' Sir Percival said angrily.
'Women don't understand business. Just sign it.'

to calm her and to find a solution to the problem of the signature. Suddenly I had the idea of writing to Mr Gilmore's partner, Mr Kyrle, and asking for his advice. In my letter I also asked him to get a messenger to bring the reply by one o'clock the next day. I then put the letter in the post-bag in the hall. Just at that moment Madame Fosco appeared and asked to speak to me in the garden. She spoke to me for a full half-hour about how much sympathy she had for me. I found this very odd indeed since she had shown very little interest in me before.

When I finally returned, I saw the Count also putting a letter in the post-bag. For some reason I decided to check my letter was properly closed, so I got it out of the bag. This was lucky, as I found the envelope had come open. How strange, I thought. Perhaps there had been something wrong with it . . .

Or perhaps . . .

No! There could be no other explanation.

6

An appointment by the lake

After dinner that evening, Laura and I went for a walk down to the lake. The atmosphere was gloomy and depressing, but at least we were alone.

'I want to have no secrets from you, Marian,' Laura said, 'but I'm sure you have already guessed what my married life is like. Sir Percival said such cruel things to me in Italy that I turned for comfort to my memories of those happy days with Walter Hartright. And I have to tell you, Marian, Sir Percival now knows that Walter is the man I loved.'

I stared at her, and what little hope I had left began to die.

'It was at a party in Rome. Some people from London said I should have drawing lessons and recommended a Mr Hartright. I could not control myself when I heard his name and my husband noticed. "So it was him, was it?" he said, with a horrible smile. "Well, we will see about Mr Hartright. You will be sorry, and so will he, to the end of your lives." And Marian, he uses this knowledge like a whip to punish me, day in, day out.'

'Oh, Laura!' I said, putting my arms around her. This was my fault – yes, my fault! I remembered the white despair of Walter's face as I told him to leave, as I tore these two young hearts apart. And I had done this for Sir Percival Glyde.

For Sir Percival Glyde.

✦ ✦ ✦

It was growing dark when we set out for home, and as we left Laura seized my arm. 'Marian, look!'

By the lake was a dark figure, half hidden by the evening mist rising off the water. We began to walk quickly.

'I'm sure it's following us,' whispered Laura. 'Is it a man or a woman?' She was shaking with fear.

'It's hard to tell in this light,' I said, then called out, 'Who's there?' There was no answer.

We hurried back through the wood, and when we reached home, I sent Laura upstairs and went to find out where everyone was. The Count and his wife, the servants, the housekeeper – all were inside. The figure by the lake was no one from the house. So who could it have been?

The next day Laura discovered she had lost her bracelet and thought she must have dropped it near the lake. She went off to look for it while I waited for the messenger from Mr Kyrle.

One o'clock came. By now I was so suspicious of everyone in the house that I decided to slip out and meet the messenger myself. Taking great care not to be seen, I went down to the main gate and a little way along the road. Soon a cab appeared. I stopped it and said, 'Are you going to Blackwater Park?'

A man put his head out and said, 'Yes, with a letter for Miss Halcombe.'

'You may give the letter to me,' I said. 'I am Miss Halcombe.' I read the letter quickly.

> *Dear Miss Halcombe — Your letter has caused me great anxiety. It seems very likely that Lady Glyde's signature is needed so that a loan of all or part of her £20,000 can be made to Sir Percival. This is almost certainly illegal, and Lady Glyde should not sign any document until I have examined it first.*
> *Sincerely, William Kyrle.*

I read this very thankfully and told the messenger to say that I understood the letter. As I spoke these words, Count Fosco came round the corner and suddenly appeared in front of me. Completely taken by surprise, I stared at him speechlessly. The messenger drove away in his cab, and the Count took my arm to walk home with me.

He talked pleasantly of this and that, and asked no questions about letters or messengers, so I assumed he had found out everything. He must have read my letter, returned it to the post-bag, and now knew that I had received an answer. There was no point in trying to deceive him so I said nothing, and just tried to seem quite cool and calm.

Back at the house we found that Sir Percival had returned, in an even worse mood than before, it seemed. When I told him Laura was out looking for her bracelet, he growled,

'Bracelet or no bracelet, I shall expect to see her in the library in half an hour.'

I turned to go into the house, but behind me heard the Count saying to Sir Percival, 'May I have five minutes' talk with you, here on the grass?'

They walked off together and I went inside to the sitting room, to think over all that had happened. Before long, however, the door opened softly and the Count looked in.

'Good news, Miss Halcombe,' he said. 'The business of the signature is put off for the moment. I'm sure you are relieved.'

He went out before I had recovered from my amazement. There could be no doubt that this change was due to his influence. His discovery of my writing to London and receiving an answer had caused him to interfere. Now there was even more to think about but, exhausted by worry and the heat of the day, my eyes closed and I fell into a little sleep.

I woke to find Laura's hand on my shoulder.

'Marian! The figure at the lake. I've just spoken to her! It's Anne Catherick. Look, she found my bracelet.'

Still half asleep, I stared at her stupidly. 'Anne Catherick?'

'Yes! I was searching in the boat-house,' Laura went on, 'when a woman in a white dress came in and said quietly, "Miss Fairlie. I have your bracelet. Your mother would not want you to lose it." I jumped up, but her voice was so kind that I wasn't afraid. I asked her how she knew my mother. She said her name was Anne Catherick and asked me if I remembered as a little girl walking with her and my mother to the school in Limmeridge one day. I did remember. Suddenly I saw that we were like each other, but her face was pale and thin and tired. It was how my face might look after a long illness. "Why do you call me Miss Fairlie?" I asked, and she answered, "Because I love the name of Fairlie and hate the name of Glyde."

'Did she say anything about your husband?' I asked.

'She said that after she wrote the letter, she did not have the courage to stay in Limmeridge to try to prevent my marriage to him. She was afraid he would find her and shut her up in the asylum again. But she was not afraid any more because she was so ill she thought she was dying. Then, Marian, she said that she and her mother knew a secret that my husband was afraid of.'

'Yes? Go on!' I said eagerly. 'What secret?'

'She was just going to tell me, when she thought she heard a noise outside. "We are not alone," she said, "someone is watching. Come here tomorrow at this time and I will tell you." Then she pushed me to one side and disappeared.'

'Oh, Laura, Laura, another chance lost! But you must keep the appointment tomorrow. It seems so important. I will follow you at a safe distance. She must not escape this time.'

We were silent for a time. Then Laura said anxiously, 'Why hasn't Sir Percival called us to the library to sign the document?'

'Oh yes! I forgot to tell you,' I said. 'Thanks to Count Fosco, the business of the signature has been postponed.'

'But why?' Laura said, amazed. 'If Sir Percival urgently needs money, how can it be postponed?'

'I heard Sir Percival's lawyer mention a second plan – to give a document promising payment in three months.'

'Oh, Marian!' she said. 'That would be such a relief.'

'Yes, it would. Let's hope that it's true.'

That evening Sir Percival was polite, even pleasant, especially to Laura. This must have been due to the Count's influence, and it worried me. What lay behind it? I was sure that Sir Percival's sudden journey yesterday had been to Welmingham, to question Mrs Catherick. What had he learnt? What were his plans? As the evening passed, I grew more and more uneasy, and I went to bed feeling very anxious about what the next day would bring.

❖ ❖ ❖

I was not wrong to be anxious. The next day Laura and I arranged that after lunch she would go alone to the boat-house, and that I would follow a little later, taking great care that Anne Catherick did not see me, in case she was frightened by the appearance of another stranger.

Sir Percival had gone out earlier in the morning and did not appear even for lunch, so it was quite easy to put our plan into action. However, when I came quietly up to the back of the boat-house, I heard no voices, no sounds of movement, nothing. Soon I was searching inside the boat-house, and softly calling Laura's name. But no one answered and no one appeared. Outside, I searched the ground for signs, and found the footprints of two people in the sand – big footprints like a man's and small footprints, which I was sure were Laura's. There was also a little hole in the sand by the wall of the boat-house.

Desperate with worry, I hurried back to the house. The first person I met was Mrs Michelson, the housekeeper.

'Do you know,' I asked, 'whether Lady Glyde has come in?'

'Yes, she has, Miss Halcombe. And I am afraid something unfortunate has happened. Lady Glyde ran upstairs in tears and Sir Percival has told me to dismiss her servant, Fanny.'

My heart sank. Fanny was Laura's personal servant from Limmeridge, and the only person in the house we both trusted.

I ran upstairs to Laura's room. Her door was shut, and there was one of Sir Percival's house servants standing in front of it.

'Move away,' I said. 'Don't you see that I want to go in?'

'But you mustn't go in,' she answered. 'I have my orders.'

Wild with anger, I turned and went downstairs to find Sir Percival. He was in the library with the Count and Countess.

'Am I to understand that your wife's room is a prison?' I asked, staring him full in the face.

'Yes, that *is* what you are to understand,' he answered.

'Take care how you treat your wife!' I shouted furiously. 'There are laws to protect women, and I will use those laws.'

Instead of answering me, he turned to the Count. The Count looked at me with his calm, cold, grey eyes. But it was the Countess who spoke.

'Thank you for your hospitality, Sir Percival,' she said suddenly. 'But I cannot remain in a house where ladies are treated as your wife and Miss Halcombe have been treated today!'

Sir Percival stared at her in shocked silence, knowing, as I did, she would not have said this without the Count's permission.

'I agree with my wife,' the Count said quietly.

Sir Percival swore, then whispered angrily, 'All right, have your own way.' With these words he left the room.

'We have made the worst-tempered man in England see reason,' said the Count. 'Thanks to your courage, Miss Halcombe, this insulting situation is now ended.'

I tried to speak normally, but could not. The Count left the library, then returned a few minutes later to say that Lady Glyde had the freedom of her own house again. Immediately I rushed upstairs to Laura's room. She was alone inside and I was in such a hurry that I did not close the door properly behind me.

'Marian!' she said thankfully. 'How did you get here?'

'It was the Count's influence, of course,' I said.

'That horrible man!' she cried. 'He's a miserable spy!'

Just then we heard a knock on the door. It was the Countess, bringing me a handkerchief I had dropped. Her face was white, and I saw in her eyes that she had been listening at the door.

'Oh, Laura,' I said when she had gone, 'you shouldn't have called the Count a spy. We shall both regret it.'

'But he *is* a spy, Marian! There was someone watching me at the lake yesterday, and it was him. He told Sir Percival, who watched and waited all morning for me and Anne Catherick. But she didn't come – I found a note from her hidden in a hole in the sand. She said she'd been followed yesterday by a fat old man.

He hadn't caught her, but she was afraid to come back this afternoon. She hid this note very early in the morning, and said she would see me again soon to tell me Sir Percival's secret.'

'What happened to the note?' I said. 'Have you got it?'

'No. While I was reading it, Sir Percival appeared. He took it from me and demanded to hear everything Anne Catherick had said. He held my arm so tightly! – look, see how he's bruised it. What could I do, Marian? I was helpless! I told him everything.'

I looked at the bruises on Laura's arm, and felt such furious hatred for Sir Percival that I dared not speak.

'But he didn't believe me,' Laura went on. 'He said he knew she had told me more and that he would lock me up until I had confessed the truth. Then he took me back to the house, gave orders for Fanny to leave, and locked me in my room. Oh, Marian, he was like a madman! What are we to do?'

'He is mad – mad with fear. He thinks you know his secret,' I said. 'I must act now to protect you – who knows how long I will be allowed to stay here?' I thought hard for a few minutes. 'I will write two letters and give them to Fanny to take with her. I can't trust the post-bag here any more. One for Mr Kyrle, telling him of your bruises and Sir Percival's violent behaviour.'

'And who is the other letter for?' asked Laura anxiously.

'For Mr Fairlie,' I said. 'Your lazy, selfish uncle. I'll make him invite you for a visit to Limmeridge, without your husband.'

I left her then and went to my room to write the letters. Fanny had already gone and was staying the night in the little hotel in the village, before beginning the long journey to Cumberland the next day. I decided I had time before dinner to walk to the village and back, so I slipped quietly out of the house and set off.

From time to time I looked behind me. Was I being followed? Or was my imagination playing tricks on me? By now I was suspicious of everything – every tiny sound, every shadow on the road, every breath of wind. Earlier, while writing the letters, I thought I had heard the rustle of a silk dress outside my door. I had even wondered if someone had been in my room, looking through the things in my desk. I hurried on, trying to put these thoughts out of my mind.

When I got to the little hotel, I saw Fanny in her room. She was very upset at leaving Laura, and started crying, but stopped when I told her that Lady Glyde and I needed her help.

'Here are two letters,' I said. 'Post the one addressed to Mr Kyrle in London tomorrow, and deliver the other to Mr Fairlie yourself when you get home to Limmeridge. Keep them safe!'

Fanny put the letters down the front of her dress. 'They'll stay there, miss,' she said, 'till I've done what you tell me.'

7

A conversation in the night

I arrived back at the house with only twenty minutes to get ready for dinner – and to slip into Laura's room to say that the letters were safely in Fanny's hands.

Laura looked pale. 'I'm not coming down to dinner,' she said. 'Sir Percival came to my door, shouting at me to tell him where Anne Catherick is.'

'At least that means he hasn't found her yet,' I said.

At dinner the Count looked hot and red in the face, and his clothes were a little untidy. Had he been out too, I wondered? He seemed troubled by some secret annoyance or anxiety, and was almost as silent as Sir Percival. At the end of the meal, when Madame Fosco and I left the table, the Count stood up too.

'Where are you going, Fosco?' Sir Percival said. 'Sit down and have another glass of wine. I want a quiet talk with you.'

'Not now, Percival. Later,' he answered.

Earlier in the day I had heard Sir Percival make the same request, and this was the second time the Count had postponed the talk. Why, I wondered? And what was it that Sir Percival wanted to discuss so urgently?

We went into the living room and Madame Fosco, usually so slow and deliberate in her movements, drank her tea at great speed and then slipped quietly out of the room. I began to leave too, but the Count stopped me, first by a request for more tea, then by asking my opinion on some music, and then by playing several noisy Italian songs on the piano. Eventually, I escaped from him and went up to Laura's room. Had she seen or heard anything of Madame Fosco, I asked? No, she had not. We talked together till ten o'clock, and then I went downstairs again to say goodnight. Sir Percival, the Count and his wife were sitting together in the living room. I noticed that Madame Fosco's face was now hot and red. Where had she been, and what had she been doing? As I looked at her, she gave a little smile, as though at some private joke.

I said goodnight to everybody, and as I left the room, I heard Sir Percival say impatiently to the Count, 'Come outside and have a smoke, Fosco.'

'With pleasure, Percival, when all the ladies have gone to bed,' replied the Count.

Up in my room, I could not stop myself thinking about this private discussion between Sir Percival and the Count, postponed all day and now, it seemed, about to take place in the silence and loneliness of the night. After a while, I went from my bedroom into my sitting room, and closed the door between the rooms. It was dark, as no candles were lit, and I looked out of the open window for some time, down into the blackness of the garden. There was a smell like rain in the still, heavy air.

Suddenly I saw two red points of light advancing in the dark and stopping below my bedroom window, inside which a candle was burning. One red point was small, the other was big. *The Count smoking a cigarette, and Sir Percival smoking a cigar, I think.* They could not see me in the darkness of my sitting room, so I waited to hear what they said.

'Why don't you come in and sit down?' Sir Percival said.

'Wait till we see that light go out,' replied the Count. 'When I know she's in bed, and I have checked the rooms on each side of the library, then we will talk.'

Such secrecy! I decided I must listen to this conversation, in spite of the Count's efforts to keep it private. The idea terrified me, but Laura's happiness – perhaps even her life – might depend on what I heard. How could I do it? I realized I could get out on to the flat verandah roof which ran past the bedrooms, about three feet below the windows. It was narrow, but there was room to move along it till I was above the library window. The Count and Sir Percival usually sat near the open window, smoking, and if they did, I would be able to hear them from above.

I went back to my bedroom, put on a long dark cloak with a hood, and put out the candle. Then, after a while, I returned to my sitting room and climbed out of the window on to the verandah roof. My heart began to beat very fast. I had to pass five windows – four were dark, but the fifth window was the Countess's room, and it looked out over the exact place above the library where I planned to sit. And there was still a light in it. I crept along the roof, then went down on my hands and knees to pass her window. As I passed, I looked up – and saw her shadow against the thin curtains at the window . . .

I stop breathing. Has she heard me? Will she look out? No,

*the shadow moves away, she's gone. Now I move to my position
at the edge of the roof and begin to listen. Are they there, or have
they gone elsewhere for their talk? Ah, I can hear the Count's
voice.*

'Miss Halcombe's light is out, the rooms next door are empty,
the only window with a light in is my wife's – so now we may
talk. We are at a serious crisis in our affairs, Percival, and we
must decide about the future tonight.'

'It's a worse crisis than you think,' growls Sir Percival.

'Listen, Percival. This is our situation. We both came to this
house in need of money and the only way of getting it was with
the help of your wife. Now what did I tell you? I told you never
to lose your temper with her, and especially never with her sister,
Miss Halcombe. And have you remembered this? Not once. Your
mad temper lost your wife's signature, lost the ready money,
made Miss Halcombe write to the lawyer for the first time—'

'First time! Has she written again?'

'Yes, she has written again today.'

*What! How does he know that? Did he follow me to the hotel?
But even if he did, he couldn't have seen the letters – they went
straight from my hand to Fanny's dress. So how does he know?*

'You're lucky,' the Count continues, 'that you have me in the
house to undo the harm that you do. Lucky that I said no when
you were mad enough to make your wife a prisoner and keep her
from Miss Halcombe. Can't you see that Miss Halcombe has the
courage and understanding of a man? How I admire that woman!
But she stands like a rock between us and that pretty little wife
of yours. Now, the money. We have obtained a loan – a horribly
expensive loan – by signing a document promising to repay it in
three months. When the time comes, is there really no way to
repay the money except by the help of your wife?'

'None.'

'What money do you actually get from your wife at present?'

'Only the income from her twenty thousand pounds.'

'Do you expect any more from your wife?'

'Absolutely nothing – except in the case of her death.'

'Aha! In the case of her death.'

A pause. It has begun to rain, and already I feel wet and cold.

Sir Percival again. 'If she leaves no children, I get her twenty thousand pounds.'

'Percival! Do you care about your wife?'

'Fosco! That's a very direct question.'

'Let's say your wife dies before the end of the summer—'

'Forget it, Fosco!'

'You would gain twenty thousand pounds.'

'Speak for yourself as well as for me, Fosco. You would also gain – *my* wife's death would be ten thousand pounds in *your* wife's pocket.'

'Percival, here is the position. If your wife lives, you pay that debt with her signature on the document. If your wife dies, you pay the debt with her death.'

The light in Madame Fosco's room goes out, and the verandah roof is now sunk in darkness. The rain continues. I listen with every nerve in my body, memorizing word after word.

'Percival, you must now leave this matter in my hands. I have more than two months to find the solution, so let's not talk about it any more. Let me help you with your other difficulty – the difficulty that seems to have the name of Anne Catherick.'

'Look, Fosco, we may be friends, but we still have our secrets. This does not concern you. Please don't ask me about it.'

'My friend, I can respect a secret. So I won't ask you to tell me. But can I help you all the same?'

'If I don't find Anne Catherick, I'm a lost man. Both she and her mother know this – this secret. It could ruin me, Fosco. Anne

Catherick has spoken to my wife and I'm sure she's told her.'

'But as your wife, surely it's in her interest to keep it a secret?'

'If she loved me, that would be true. But she's in love with someone she met before we married, a drawing teacher called Walter Hartright. And who helped Anne Catherick escape from the asylum? Hartright. Who saw her again in Cumberland? Hartright. He knows the secret, and my wife knows the secret. If they get together, they will use it against me.'

'Yes, yes, I see. Where is Mr Hartright?'

'Out of the country. He sailed for America.'

'Don't worry, then. I will deal with him if he ever comes back. Depend on it. But first we must find Anne Catherick. What about her mother? Can she be trusted?'

'It's in her interest not to tell anyone the secret.'

'Good. Now, how will I recognize Anne Catherick?'

'Easily. She's the pale, sickly likeness of my wife.'

A noise as a chair is pushed back. The Count has jumped to his feet and is walking about. He seems amazed.

'What!!! Are she and your wife related to each other?'

'Not at all.'

'And yet so alike? Well, I will know her when I see her.'

'What the devil are you laughing about, Fosco?'

'Just a thought, my good friend, just a thought. But enough for tonight. You will pay the debt and find Anne Catherick. I promise you. You can put your mind at rest, Percival.'

Not another word is spoken. I hear the library door close. I am wet to the skin, stiff and aching with the cold. At first I can't move, but slowly, painfully, I creep back to my window and climb in. As I fall on the floor, I hear the clock strike a quarter past one. Time passes. Somehow I manage to get up and put on dry clothes. I am burning hot – and shivering with cold. I know I must write down what I have heard, so I find paper and pen and

The Count has jumped to his feet and is walking about.
He seems amazed.

write without stopping. The fever rises in me, burning, burning. I open the window for cool air . . .

Eight o'clock. Bright sunshine, which hammers at my eyes. My head aches, my bones ache, my skin burns, yet I cannot stop shivering. I lie down to sleep, my writing finished, and in my fever I see Count Fosco come into my room and read the pages I have written. He smiles. I am helpless – unable to move, speak, breathe . . . and I sink into the long, black night of illness . . .

8

Fever

While I lay unconscious in my illness, I knew nothing, of course, of the events happening around me. It was only much later that I learnt from other people what had happened.

When I eventually returned to Limmeridge, Fanny told me about the letters and the night she had left Blackwater.

'You left me at about seven, miss, and at nine o'clock I had another visitor – the Countess! Yes, I was so surprised. But she was very kind. She saw that I was upset at leaving and insisted on having some tea with me. So I drank my tea, and five minutes later I fainted – for the first time in my life! When I woke up, it was about half an hour later. A lady from the hotel was looking after me as the Countess had had to go home. I checked the letters in my dress, miss, and they were both there, quite safe.

'And just as you told me, in London I posted the letter to Mr Kyrle, and as soon as I got to Limmeridge, I delivered the other letter personally to Mr Fairlie. I told him all about being dismissed by Sir Percival and everything, and what had happened at the hotel, but, well, he didn't seem very interested, miss.'

That last piece of information did not surprise me in the least. Had Laura's uncle ever been interested in anybody except himself? When I went to talk to him, he was full of excuses.

'My nerves, dear Marian, remember my nerves! Yes, of course I will tell you about the letters, but please don't get excited and go around banging doors! Try to stay calm.'

'I suppose my letter about Laura upset you,' I said.

'Of course it did, dear Marian! What was I to do? You told me Laura needed to escape from her husband and to come to Limmeridge. But suppose Sir Percival had come after her? Think of the noise, the arguments, the banging of doors! That's why I wrote to you, to beg you to come here first by yourself, to talk the matter over with me.'

I never saw that letter, of course, as it arrived at Blackwater when I was unconscious with fever.

'And Mr Kyrle wrote to you as well, didn't he?' I said.

'Yes. He wrote to say he had received an envelope addressed to him in your handwriting, but which contained only a plain piece of paper without a word on it. He had written to you about it, and had received no reply. Why he expected *me* to explain this mystery, I had no idea. And that's what I told him.'

So helpful, I thought bitterly. But there was no point in saying anything. 'And were you surprised not to hear from me again?'

'Indeed I was, until my sister's foreign husband, that extraordinary Count Fosco, came to see me. Such a huge man!' said Mr Fairlie, his eyes closing at the memory. 'But surprisingly quiet on his feet. Anyway, he explained how ill you were, dear Marian, which was why you hadn't replied to my letter. I was extremely shocked and sorry to hear about your illness. But the Count did talk so much – I thought he would never leave!'

'And he persuaded you to write to Laura,' I said, trying to keep my voice calm and quiet.

'Yes, he urged me – in fact, practically *ordered* me – to invite Laura here at once. She was too nervous and upset to be of any use to you in the sick-room, he said, and the situation with Sir Percival was growing more dangerous every day. There was no trouble with the journey, because he and his wife had just rented a house in London. So Laura could travel up to London, stay the night with them, and travel on to Cumberland the next day.'

'So you wrote the letter and gave it to him,' I said.

'Where was the harm in it? In any case, I never for a moment thought that Laura would leave you alone when you were so ill. And how was I to know what shocking event was about to take place? No one could possibly say that I was to blame . . .'

✤ ✤ ✤

I know now exactly who was to blame, but it took quite a time to put all the different pieces of information together. When I first began to be aware of my surroundings again during my recovery, I knew nothing, of course, about the letters. I knew only that I was not in my usual bedroom and there was a foreign lady looking after me. I had no idea who she was and she would not answer any of my questions. So I was very relieved a few days later when the familiar face of Mrs Michelson appeared.

'Oh, Mrs Michelson,' I said, 'I'm so glad to see you. Please tell me what's been happening.'

'You've had typhus fever, Miss Halcombe. You've been very ill. But you're getting stronger now, I'm happy to say.'

'Typhus! No wonder I feel so weak. And my sister, Lady Glyde – I do hope she didn't catch the infection?'

'No, no, she didn't.'

Mrs Michelson would not look me in the face, and I began to feel worried. Was she afraid to tell me something?

'Is my sister ill? Please, Mrs Michelson, I must know!'

'No, she's not ill. But . . . but she's not here. She went away yesterday to London, and is going on to Limmeridge today.'

I stared at her. Laura gone? I could not believe it. What did it mean? Had something terrible happened? I remembered the conversation I heard during the night on the verandah roof, and my heart filled with fear.

'And Sir Percival . . .?' I could not finish my question.

'Sir Percival left the house last night, to go abroad,' she said. 'The Count and Countess have gone to London, and the servants have all been dismissed, except for a cook and the gardener. You and I are the only people living in the house, Miss Halcombe.'

The shock of this news was so great that I felt faint. Mrs Michelson hurried to fetch me a glass of water.

'Oh, Miss Halcombe, I'm sorry,' she said. 'Try not to worry. You must rest now, and try to sleep a little.'

Later, when I felt stronger, we talked again. 'Tell me everything you can remember, from the day I fell ill,' I begged Mrs Michelson. 'I must know what happened.'

'Well, Miss Halcombe, on that first morning a servant found you, lying on your bed in a fever, holding a pen tightly in your hand. The doctor was called at once, a Mr Dawson, who said you were very ill. The Countess and I acted as your nurses – Lady Glyde wanted to help, but she was so upset at seeing you unconscious that she couldn't stop crying.

'Sir Percival and the Count were concerned about you too, though they seemed worried about something else as well. In fact, the Count spent three days down by the lake, at that old boat-house, and I remember he came in once when I was going through the hall. Sir Percival came rushing out of the library, saying, "Have you found her?" I didn't hear the answer and I have no idea who they were talking about.'

I had a very good idea who they were talking about, but it was obvious that Mrs Michelson didn't, so I said nothing.

'Your fever got worse,' Mrs Michelson went on. 'The Count said we needed a nurse to help us, so Madame Fosco took the train to London and came back with Mrs Rubelle.'

'Is that the foreign lady who was looking after me before you appeared, Mrs Michelson?' I asked.

'Yes, that's right. She didn't say very much, but she was a capable nurse. I had no complaints about her work. Mr Dawson, the doctor, was suspicious of her because she was recommended by the Count, and he didn't like the Count at all.'

'Why was that?' I asked.

'The Count had a lot of medical knowledge, you see, and he was always suggesting to Mr Dawson ways of reducing your fever. Mr Dawson called it interference and got quite angry about it. But in fact, miss, the Count recognized you had typhus fever before Mr Dawson did. He – the Count, that is – went away to London for a week, and when he came back, he took one look at you and said "Typhus". Mr Dawson sent to London for another doctor, who came and said the same thing. Then we had a very worrying ten days, when your life was in danger, but at last the doctor said you were through the worst and with good nursing care you would recover. Lady Glyde was so overcome by this happy news that she became ill herself and had to be put to bed.'

'My sister has always had delicate health,' I said.

'Yes, she's not strong. Anyway, Miss Halcombe, it was at this point that disturbing things started to happen. First, the Count and Mr Dawson argued again so fiercely that Mr Dawson left, saying he refused to offer his services any more. Next, Sir Percival told me that he was going to close the house. As soon as you and Lady Glyde were able to travel, he said, you would be going away for a change of air. He told me to dismiss all the servants, except a girl to do the cooking, and a gardener. Imagine! Just like that! I tell you, Miss Halcombe, if I hadn't felt so sorry for you and Lady Glyde, I would have resigned at once!

'The last thing was very strange indeed,' said Mrs Michelson, shaking her head. 'Sir Percival said that you and Lady Glyde would benefit from a stay at the seaside town of Torquay. He told me to go there to look for a suitable house to rent, and told me how much money I could pay. Well, I knew it wasn't enough, and I wish now that I hadn't gone, but he was my employer so I thought I had to obey his orders. I returned yesterday, after two days away, and told Sir Percival that it was impossible to find a house at such a low rent. Sir Percival showed no interest in my news at all. He just said that the Count and Countess had left Blackwater Park for their new house in London.'

Mrs Michelson looked at me anxiously. 'I think you'll find the next part of the story very upsetting,' she said. 'Poor Lady Glyde was cruelly deceived by her husband.'

'You don't surprise me,' I murmured. 'Please go on.'

'After seeing Sir Percival, I went upstairs to see you and Lady Glyde. Your sister, though still very weak, was feeling better and wanted to get up and go and visit you in your room. I helped her to dress and as we went down the passage, we met Sir Percival.

'"If you're going to see your sister, you won't find her," Sir Percival says. "She left the house yesterday with Fosco and his wife. She decided to go with them to London, on her way to Limmeridge. Mrs Rubelle went too, to look after her on the journey. You can look in her room if you don't believe me."

'I was shocked and amazed by this, and Lady Glyde's face went as white as a sheet. She almost ran down the passage and threw open the door to your room. It was empty.

'Then she cries out to Sir Percival, "Marian was much too ill to travel. Even if she did go, she would never leave without saying goodbye to me first. And why would she go to Limmeridge alone, leaving me here at Blackwater Park?"

'"Because your uncle won't receive you till he has seen your sister first," says Sir Percival. "Have you forgotten the letter he wrote to her at the beginning of her illness?"

'All through this interview, Miss Halcombe, I thought Sir Percival seemed very strange – jumpy and nervous, not at all his usual self. And now he just turned and walked away. Lady Glyde was shaking with fear, and looked at me with terror in her eyes. "Something's happened to my sister. I must follow her – I must see that she's alive and well with my own eyes. Please, Mrs Michelson, come down with me to Sir Percival. Stay with me, please!" She held my arm so tightly that I had to go with her.

'Sir Percival was in the dining room, drinking. He drank at least four glasses of wine while we were in there, Miss Halcombe. Lady Glyde was very brave, I thought. She said, "If my sister is well enough to travel, then so am I. Please allow me to follow her at once by the afternoon train."

'Sir Percival was so rude and rough with her. "You can go tomorrow," he said. "I'll write to Fosco. He can meet you at the station and you'll stay at his house overnight."

'Lady Glyde's hand began to tremble violently on my arm. "I would rather not stay at the Count's house," she said.

'Sir Percival then got very angry. "Why not?" he shouted. "What's wrong with sleeping at your aunt's house? Your sister slept there last night to break her journey, and so will you. That's what your uncle, Mr Fairlie, wants you to do as well. Here – there's a letter from him. I forgot to send it up to you."

'Poor Lady Glyde was shaking so much that she gave me the letter to read to her. It was very short. I remember it, word for word: *Dear Laura, please come whenever you like. Break the journey by sleeping at your aunt's house. Sorry to hear of Marian's illness. Your fond uncle, Frederick Fairlie.*

'Lady Glyde didn't try to argue any more, and we went back upstairs. It seemed quite a sensible plan to me, Miss Halcombe, and I couldn't understand why Lady Glyde was so terrified of Count Fosco. She walked up and down her room, whispering, "Poor Marian – in that horrible man's power! I must find her, even if I have to follow her to Count Fosco's house."

'The next day I helped Lady Glyde get ready and went with her to the station. "If Marian has already left for Limmeridge, I won't stay at the Count's house," she told me. "I'll go and stay with Mrs Vesey, my old governess." As the train pulled away, I saw her pale, frightened face at the window. I felt so sad for her.

'Then I came back here. Imagine my surprise, Miss Halcombe, when I saw Mrs Rubelle walking in the garden! "What are *you* doing here?" I said. "You went to London with the Foscos and Miss Halcombe!" And then it all came out. You were still in the house. While I was out of the way in Torquay, they moved you to a room in an unused part of the house and kept you hidden. You must have been in a very deep sleep when they moved you. Perhaps they drugged you – I don't know. Then Sir Percival appeared and gave me this explanation. It was all for his wife's own good, he said. She needed a change of air, and would not have gone to Limmeridge if she had known that you were still in the house. He spoke in such a violent, angry way that I did not dare to express my opinion.

'So you see, Miss Halcombe, that was how poor Lady Glyde was deceived. It was wicked and cruel. I would have resigned my position immediately, but Sir Percival told me that Mrs Rubelle was leaving and there would be no one to look after you if I left too. So, naturally, I stayed. Sir Percival left last night, as I told you. The gardener said he seemed half mad. He called for his

carriage, and drove away like an escaped criminal, saying his
house was a prison and he would never return to it. I hope and
pray, Miss Halcombe, that I never see that man again.'

Poor Laura – how she must have suffered! There was nothing
I could do. I could not go after her as I was too weak even to
stand. I hoped desperately that she had found out about the
deception and would write soon to tell me that she was safe.

❖ ❖ ❖

A letter came a few days later, but it was not for me, and not
from Laura. It was for Mrs Michelson from Madame Fosco.

Mrs Michelson came into my room with the letter in her hand.
Mr Dawson, who had agreed to be my doctor again now that the
Count had gone, was behind her. I took one look at both their
faces, and sat up in bed, terrified.

'What is it?' I gasped. 'You have some dreadful news for me.
I can see it in your faces.'

Mrs Michelson sat down on the edge of the bed and took my
hand. 'Your poor, dear sister, Lady Glyde . . .' she began.

The room began to darken around me, as though night was
falling, and the words seemed to come from a great distance.

'. . . was taken seriously ill when she arrived at her aunt's
house in London, and died the next day, very suddenly. She is
to be buried at Limmeridge, in her mother's grave.'

❖ ❖ ❖

Kind Mrs Michelson nursed me through my second illness, with
Mr Dawson's help. I was not able to travel for more than three
weeks, but eventually I found the strength to leave that hated
house and return to Limmeridge. Mrs Michelson and I travelled
together to London, where I went to see Mr Kyrle. To him I
revealed the terrible suspicions in my mind about the
circumstances of my sister's death. He was most concerned and
promised to make enquiries for me.

I went on to Limmeridge House and a few days later Mr Kyrle wrote to me there. He had taken statements from several witnesses, he said, and was convinced that nothing suspicious had happened. He sent copies of the statements for my information. This was the one by the Count's cook, Mrs Hester Pinhorn:

I was recently employed as a cook by the Count and Countess Fosco at 5 Forest Road, St John's Wood. One day near the end of July, the Countess's niece, Lady Glyde, arrived at the house. She immediately fell ill. I saw her lying on the sofa, her face all white. I ran out for a doctor and came back with Mr Goodricke. He examined her and said she had a very serious heart disease. During the night she got worse. Then, at about five o'clock the next day, she lost consciousness. The doctor went in and, after putting his hand on her heart, announced that she was dead. He said that, as the Count was a foreigner, he himself would go to record the death at the district office. The Count and Countess were very badly affected by the lady's death. The lady's husband was abroad, so they arranged the funeral themselves, which took place in Cumberland.

I was still very weak from my long illness, and despair nearly overtook me at this point. I had no friend to turn to, and no idea what to do next. I went every day to the churchyard, to put flowers on the grave and to read again those sad, sad words.

IN LOVING MEMORY OF LAURA, LADY GLYDE
WIFE OF SIR PERCIVAL GLYDE, OF BLACKWATER PARK, HAMPSHIRE
BORN 27TH MARCH 1829
DIED 25TH JULY 1850

9

The gravestone

On 13th October 1850 I left the wild forests of Central America and returned to England. I had escaped death by disease, death by war, and death by drowning, and hoped that these experiences had strengthened me to face my future – a future without Laura Fairlie. I still remembered her as Laura Fairlie, and could not think of her by her husband's name.

The first thing I did was to visit my mother and sister in their Hampstead cottage. The joy of our meeting, however, soon turned to sadness. I have no secrets from my mother, and when I saw the loving pity in her eyes, I feared the worst.

The news was soon told. I tried hard not to let my sorrow spoil the happiness of my return for my mother and sister, but by the third day I knew I had to go away alone for a while.

'Let me go up to Limmeridge,' I begged my mother. 'I can bear it better when I have seen her grave.'

It was a warm autumn afternoon when I arrived at the station and walked down the familiar road, seeing in the distance the high white walls of Limmeridge House. In the churchyard I found the grave and knelt down beside the gravestone, closing my eyes.

Oh my love! My love! My dear, dear love!

Hours passed, and the evening sunlight threw long shadows among the sleeping places of the dead. I had lost all sense of time,

kneeling there. Then, in the silence, I heard the soft sound of
footsteps on the grass.

I looked up.

Beyond me, standing together by the churchyard wall, were
two women, their veils down, hiding their faces. They were
looking towards the grave, looking towards *me*.

Two.

They came closer, and stopped. One of them lifted her veil,
and in the still evening light I saw the face of Marian
Halcombe. A changed face. Thin and pale, full of pain and fear.

The woman with the veiled face came towards me slowly.
Marian Halcombe sank to her knees, murmuring, 'Oh God, help
him! Please, please help him, God!'

The veiled woman came on, slowly and silently. I looked at
her – at her, and at no one else, from that moment. She had
possession of me, body and soul. She stopped by the side of the
gravestone, and we stood face to face with the grave between us.

'Oh God, help him, help him!'

The woman lifted her veil.

In Loving Memory of Laura, Lady Glyde . . .

Laura, Lady Glyde, was standing by the gravestone, looking
at me over her grave.

✢ ✢ ✢

A life suddenly changed. A new future before me, like the sunlit
view from a mountain top. I leave my story in the quiet shadow
of Limmeridge church, and begin again, one week later, in the
noise and rush of a London street.

I have rented rooms under a different name. Marian and
Laura, using the same name, are said to be my sisters. I earn our
bread by doing drawings for cheap magazines. We employ no
servant; my elder sister, Marian, does the housework with her
own hands. Marian and I are known to be the friends of mad

Anne Catherick (address unknown), who falsely claims the identity of Lady Glyde. To the rest of the world, Laura, Lady Glyde, is dead. Dead to her uncle, who has refused to recognize her; dead to the lawyers, who have passed her fortune to her husband and aunt.

Laura, Lady Glyde, was standing by the gravestone, looking at me over her grave.

But to Marian and me she is alive! Penniless and sadly changed – her beauty faded, her mind confused – but alive, with her poor drawing teacher to fight her battles and to win her way back to the world of living beings. She is mine at last – mine to support, to protect, to defend. And mine to love.

10

The rescue

At the first opportunity we had, Marian told me everything that had happened to her and Laura. The hardest part for her was after she had returned to Limmeridge House.

'I was in despair, Walter,' she said. 'Mr Kyrle's investigation was finished, and had shown nothing, he said. Mr Fairlie was no help at all – I heard that he didn't even leave his room to go to the funeral! But he did show me a letter he'd received from Count Fosco, which contained news of Anne Catherick. The Count said that Anne Catherick had been found and put back in the asylum from which she had escaped. But because she hated Sir Percival and wanted to make trouble for him, she was now claiming that she was not Anne Catherick at all, but Lady Glyde. The Count warned Mr Fairlie that if she escaped again, she might try to annoy members of Lady Glyde's family.

'I wasn't well enough to do anything for about a month after returning to Limmeridge, but when I felt stronger, I decided to make some investigations myself. First, I planned to visit the asylum in London and talk to poor Anne Catherick, to find out why she was claiming to be Laura. I knew the address because you had given it to me, all those months ago.

'Well, Walter, you can guess what's coming, I'm sure. The director of the asylum, who seemed an honest person, told me that Anne Catherick had been brought back on 27th July. He was puzzled by some odd personal changes in her, but assumed they were caused by her mental illness. He then called a nurse to take me to Anne Catherick, who was walking in the gardens.

'Imagine the shock, Walter – seeing my dead sister walking towards me in that garden! We just ran into each other's arms, unable to say a word. How the nurse stared at us!'

'I think I know how you must have felt,' I said. 'I shall never forget in the churchyard at Limmeridge . . . But tell me, however did you get Laura out of the asylum?'

'Bribery, Walter. I didn't want to risk a legal battle and all the delay that would involve, so I persuaded the nurse that a terrible mistake had been made and she would be doing a good thing in helping Anne Catherick escape. And I offered her £400. The plan went smoothly, and by early afternoon the next day Laura and I were on the train to Cumberland.'

'And Laura?' I asked. 'What actually happened on the day she left Blackwater Park and came to London?'

Marian sighed. 'Oh, Walter, it's not at all clear. Poor Laura's mind is so confused now that her memory of events is very unreliable. She can't even remember the date she left Blackwater. All she has been able to tell me is this. The Count met her at the station, and said that I was still in London and that he would take her to see me at once. She doesn't remember where the cab went, but it was clearly not to his house in St John's Wood. She was taken to a house in a narrow street, where people came and went, asking her questions she didn't understand. At this point the Count told her I was now very ill; she was so frightened by this news she nearly fainted. Someone then gave her a glass of water, which she said tasted odd – and after that she lost consciousness.'

'Poor, poor Laura,' I murmured.

'She woke up,' Marian continued, 'in the asylum, unable to leave, unable to make contact with the outside world. She was called by Anne Catherick's name and found she was wearing clothes with Anne Catherick's name on them. She was told Lady Glyde was dead and buried, and that she was Anne Catherick, Anne Catherick, Anne Catherick . . . Day in, day out, from 27th July to 15th October, she was made to feel that she was mad. It's hardly surprising her mind is so confused now.'

'And what happened at Limmeridge?' I asked.

Marian turned her face away. 'I can't bear to think about it,' she said. 'The worst part was taking Laura into Mr Fairlie's room. He looked straight into Laura's face and said, "My niece is buried in Limmeridge churchyard. I don't recognize this woman. Remove her from my house before I call on the law to protect me." Even the servants were doubtful about her identity, because she was so much changed and so confused by her experiences. Perhaps people would have been persuaded if we'd stayed longer, but I didn't dare risk it. At any minute the people from the asylum might come looking for us, so I decided to return to London at once and hide. Then, as we were passing the churchyard, Laura insisted on a last look at her mother's grave. And . . . well, that moment changed our three lives.'

'I think God was guiding Laura's footsteps,' I said.

How well I remember that day – that moment when Laura laid her poor head innocently and trustingly on my shoulder, and said, 'They have tried to make me forget everything, Walter, but I remember Marian, and I remember *you*.'

❖ ❖ ❖

The plot against Laura was now clear. Anne Catherick had been taken into Count Fosco's house as Lady Glyde, and Lady Glyde had taken the dead woman's place in the asylum. It was also clear

that the three of us could expect no mercy from Count Fosco and
Sir Percival, who between them had gained £30,000 from the plot.
They would do everything in their power to prevent their crime
being discovered, and would hunt for their victim to separate her
from her only friends – Marian and myself. This is why I had
chosen a poor and crowded part of London to live in. It is easier
to hide in a place where people are always coming and going.

Our life quickly took on a regular pattern – work, watching
out for our enemies, and care of Laura, whom we surrounded
with a gentle, protective love, helping her slowly but steadily to
recover her balance of mind and her self-confidence.

Meanwhile, Marian and I began the battle. We studied the
statements that Mr Kyrle had taken from witnesses – the doctor,
and the servants and cook in Count Fosco's house. I obtained a
copy of Lady Glyde's death certificate, and Marian wrote to Mrs
Michelson, who replied, saying that she could not remember the
exact date of Laura's departure from Blackwater Park. Nor could
she remember when the letter announcing Laura's death, which
was undated, had arrived from Madame Fosco.

I also arranged to visit Mr Kyrle, to ask for his help. After
listening to my long explanation, the lawyer shook his head.

'My legal opinion, Mr Hartright, is that you won't win this
case in a court of law. I accept, of course, that the identity of Lady
Glyde as a living person is a proved fact to Miss Halcombe and
yourself. But there is no evidence. If you could prove that the date
on the death certificate was *earlier* than the date of Lady Glyde's
journey to London, then you might have a case.'

As I left, he gave me a letter that had been delivered to him
for Marian, and told me, in answer to my question, that Sir
Percival Glyde had returned to London.

Outside in the street I soon noticed two men following me,
and realized too late that the Count's spies must have been

watching the lawyer's office, in the hope that Marian or I would go there. I went home by a very long route and managed to lose them, but it was a warning to me to be more careful.

Marian was very worried when I told her about the two men. Then I gave her the letter. She recognized the writing instantly.

'It's from Count Fosco.'

Dear and admirable woman, do not be afraid! Stay hidden, with your gentle companion, and nothing will happen to you. Challenge nothing, threaten nobody. Do not, I beg you, force me into action. If Mr Hartright returns to England, do not speak to him. If he crosses my path, he is a lost man. F.

'Walter!' Marian said, her eyes flashing with anger. 'If ever the Count and Sir Percival are at your mercy and you must spare one of them, don't let it be the Count.'

'I'll keep this letter to remind me when the time comes,' I said. 'But tomorrow I will go to Blackwater, to try and find out the date of Laura's journey to London. It's the one weak point in their plot.'

'You mean that perhaps Laura did not leave for London until after the date on the death certificate?'

'Exactly. I think she left on 26th July. The Director of the asylum said she was taken there on the 27th. I doubt if they could have kept her drugged more than one night. We know from Mrs Michelson that Sir Percival left on the same day as Laura. I'll ask everyone in the village if they remember when he left.'

'And if that fails?'

'If that fails, Marian, I'll force a confession from Sir Percival. We have one weapon against him – his secret. Anne Catherick said that if his secret was known, it would ruin him. I intend to find out that secret. The woman in white, though dead in her grave, is still with us and is showing us the way!'

11

The investigation

The story of my first enquiries in Hampshire is soon told. Not a single person in the village of Blackwater could remember exactly when Sir Percival Glyde had left. Even the gardener at the house could only say it was some time in the last ten days of July.

'So, on to the next plan,' I said to Marian back in London, 'which is to pursue the secret. I need to talk to Anne Catherick's mother, but first I must find out something about her from Mrs Clements, Anne's friend. But how do I find Mrs Clements?'

Marian had the answer to that. 'You remember the farm she and Anne stayed at near Limmeridge? We'll write to them – they might know Mrs Clements' address.'

We were lucky. The farmer's wife did know the address, and wrote back by return to tell us. It was in London, not far from our rooms, and the next morning I was knocking at the door.

Mrs Clements was anxious to know if I had brought her any news of Anne, and very sad to learn that I had not. However, she was willing to tell me everything she knew.

'After leaving Limmeridge, sir,' she said, 'Anne and I went to live in the north east of England, and that's when Anne started to suffer from heart disease. She wasn't at all well, but she insisted on travelling to Hampshire, because she wanted to speak to Lady Glyde. So we went there and stayed in a village near Blackwater – not too close as Anne was so frightened of Sir Percival.

'Each time Anne went to the lake to try to speak to Lady

Glyde, I followed her at a distance. But the long walks made her so exhausted that she became ill again, so finally I went to the lake in her place to meet Lady Glyde. She didn't come that day, but a very fat man came instead with a message from her. The message was that we should return to London immediately, as Sir Percival would certainly find us if we stayed longer. Lady Glyde was going to London herself very soon and if we sent her our address, she would contact us.'

'But she didn't, did she?' I said, thinking how cleverly Count Fosco had lied to this kind woman.

'No, sir. I found lodgings and sent the address to Lady Glyde, but after two weeks we'd still heard nothing. Then one day a lady called in a cab. She said she came from Lady Glyde, who was staying at a hotel and wanted to arrange an interview with Anne. I agreed to go with this lady to make the arrangement, leaving Anne alone in our lodgings. But it was a wicked plot, sir. On the way the lady stopped the cab, saying she just had to collect something from a shop and would I wait for a few minutes. She never came back, sir. I waited for some time, and then I hurried home – and found Anne gone. Just disappeared.'

I asked Mrs Clements to describe this 'lady', and it seemed clear from her description that it was Madame Fosco. So I now knew how the Count had got Anne Catherick to London and separated her from Mrs Clements.

'I never found out what happened to Anne,' Mrs Clements said sadly. 'I made enquiries. I even wrote to her mother, but she didn't know anything. I miss poor Anne so much. She was like a daughter to me, you see, sir.'

'And I'm sure you were a kind mother to her,' I said. 'A better mother than her own mother.'

'That wasn't difficult,' said Mrs Clements. 'Mrs Catherick is a hard woman. She seemed to hate the child, and was only too

pleased when I offered to bring her up. Then one day she took
Anne to Limmeridge to stay with a sister, and after that she kept
Anne from me. I didn't see Anne again till she escaped from the
asylum – with your help, sir. And then she was always talking
about a secret her mother had which could ruin Sir Percival. But
you know, sir, I don't think Anne really knew what this secret
was. If she had known, I'm sure she would have told me.'

I had wondered about that myself, and now I tried to turn the
conversation on to Mrs Catherick.

'Did you know Mrs Catherick before Anne was born?'

'Yes, for about four months. We were neighbours in
Welmingham. Mr and Mrs Catherick had just got married, and
Mr Catherick had a job as clerk at Welmingham church. Before
that, Mrs Catherick had been a servant at a large house. She was
a selfish, heartless woman, and treated her poor husband very
badly. Before long, there was a lot of talk about her and a young
gentleman, who was staying at a hotel nearby. And Mr Catherick
told my husband that he'd found expensive presents, gold rings
and suchlike, hidden in his wife's drawer.'

'And who was this gentleman?' I asked.

'You know him, sir. And so did my poor dear Anne.'

'Sir Percival Glyde?' My heart began to beat faster. Was I
getting close to the secret?

'That's right. His father had recently died abroad, and Sir
Percival had just arrived in the neighbourhood. People thought,
you see, that maybe Mrs Catherick had known Sir Percival
before, and had married Mr Catherick just to save her
reputation, because of, well, you know . . . Anyway, one night
Mr Catherick found his wife whispering with Sir Percival outside
the vestry of the church. They had a fight, but Sir Percival beat
him and Mr Catherick left the village, never to return again. And
in spite of all the talk in the village, Mrs Catherick stayed. She

said she was innocent and that no one would drive her away. But most people thought that the money she lived on came from Sir Percival.'

The secret was here somewhere. But where? That Sir Percival was Anne's father was hardly a secret since everyone already thought that. No, there was another mystery somewhere.

'And what did you think, Mrs Clements?'

'Well, sir, if you worked out time and place, it was obvious that Mr Catherick wasn't Anne's father. But Anne wasn't at all like Sir Percival; and nor was she like her mother.'

I wondered about the house where Mrs Catherick had worked as a servant. Perhaps I would make some enquiries later.

'You've been very kind, Mrs Clements,' I said, 'answering all my questions. One last request. Will you tell me Mrs Catherick's address? I have to find out this secret, and only she can tell me.'

Mrs Clements gave me the address, but shook her head. 'Take care, sir. She's an awful woman. You don't know her as I do.'

✣ ✣ ✣

Back at our rooms I announced my intention to Marian of going to Welmingham. She was very uneasy about the plan.

'Are you sure it's wise, Walter? Sir Percival is a violent man.'

'I'm more afraid for you and Laura,' I said, 'left alone in London, with the Count as your enemy.'

We arranged to write to each other every day; and if no letter came from her, I would take the first train back to London.

✣ ✣ ✣

Three days later I was standing in Mrs Catherick's sitting room, face to face with a grey-haired woman, dressed in black silk. Her dark eyes looked straight at me with a hard, cold stare.

'You say you have come to speak to me about my daughter,' she said. 'Please say what you have to say.'

Her voice was as hard as the expression in her eyes. She

pointed to a chair, and looked at me carefully as I sat down.

'You know,' I said, 'that your daughter is lost?'

'I know that perfectly well.'

'Don't you worry that she might not be just lost, but that she might have met with her death?'

'Yes. Have you come to tell me that she is dead?'

'I have.'

'Why?'

She asked that extraordinary question without the slightest change in her voice, face, or manner. I might have been talking about the death of a cat in the street.

'I thought Anne's mother might be interested in knowing if she was alive or dead.'

'Just so,' she said. 'But what is your interest in her, or in me? Have you no other reason for coming here?'

'Yes, I do,' I said. 'Your daughter's death has caused someone I love to be harmed – by a man called Sir Percival Glyde.'

She did not react at all at the mention of his name.

'I want to make him confess to his crime. You know certain things about him from the time when your husband was the church clerk. I want you to tell me about them.'

At last I saw the anger burning in her eyes.

'What do you know about those events?'

'Everything that Mrs Clements could tell me.'

'Mrs Clements is a foolish woman.' She bit back her anger, and her lips curled in an unpleasant little smile. 'Ah, I begin to understand. *You* want your revenge on Sir Percival Glyde, and you want *my* help. That's why you've come here. Well, you don't know me. I've spent years getting back my reputation in this village. Now everyone respects me. I won't help you.'

'If you're afraid of Sir Percival, that's quite understandable,' I said. 'He's a powerful man, and comes from a great family—'

To my amazement, she suddenly burst out laughing.

'From a great family! Yes, indeed! Especially from his mother's side,' she said with disgust.

Whatever did she mean by that, I wondered?

'The secret between you and Sir Percival was not guilty love,' I insisted. 'It was something else that brought you and him to those stolen meetings outside the vestry of the church.'

As I said the words 'vestry of the church', I saw a wave of terror pass across her face.

'Go!' she said. 'And never come back. Unless' – and she gave a slow, cruel smile – 'unless you bring news of his death.'

✤ ✤ ✤

It was now late, and I made my way to the nearest hotel. There was much to think about. Why should mention of the church vestry cause terror? Why the disgust at Sir Percival's family, especially his mother? Was there something unusual about his parents' marriage? Perhaps the local marriage register was kept in the vestry of Welmingham church . . .

The next day I went to the church. I had been aware of being followed the previous evening, and now I caught sight of the same two men I had seen outside Mr Kyrle's office in London. It seemed that Sir Percival had expected me to visit Mrs Catherick, and was now expecting me to visit Welmingham church – proof, surely, that my investigation was going in the right direction.

I found the church clerk, who fetched his keys and took me to the vestry. It could only be entered from the outside of the church, and the clerk had great difficulty opening the lock, which was very old. Once inside, I asked to see the marriage register. It was kept in a cupboard which could easily be forced open.

'Is that a safe enough place to keep the register?' I said.

'Safe enough,' the clerk said. 'A copy is kept by a lawyer in the next village – Mr Wansborough's office in Knowlesbury.'

I worked backwards in the register from Sir Percival's year of birth and there, under September of the previous year, squashed into a small space at the bottom of the page, was the record of the marriage of Sir Felix Glyde and Cecilia Elster of Knowlesbury. Just the usual information. Nothing apparently peculiar about Sir Percival's mother. The secret seemed further away than ever.

But on to Knowlesbury, and Mr Wansborough's office – a five-mile walk, but possible to get there and back by the end of the day. It was worth checking the copy of the register, and perhaps the lawyer would know something that might be useful.

12

The secret

Sir Percival's spies attacked me on the road to Knowlesbury. One of them came up beside me, and bumped into me with his shoulder. I pushed him away, hard, and he immediately shouted for help. The other man ran up and the two of them held me between them. The first man accused me of attacking him, and they said they would take me to the police station in the town.

What could I do? I couldn't fight both of them and hope to get away, so I had to go with them.

At the police station the first man accused me of a violent attack, and the second man said he was a witness. I was locked up until the next magistrate's court, which was three days away. I could be released on bail, I was told, but how could I, a total stranger in the town, find a responsible person willing to pay money for my temporary freedom? The whole plan was now clear – to get me out of the way for three days, while Sir Percival did whatever was necessary to prevent his secret being discovered.

At first I was too angry to think clearly. Then I remembered Mr Dawson, the doctor. I had been to his house on my previous visit to Blackwater, so I knew his address. I wrote him a letter, explaining what had happened and begging for his help, and then asked for a messenger to deliver it. Two hours later the good doctor appeared, paid the required money and I was set free.

There was no time to lose. The news of my being free would doubtless reach Sir Percival within hours. I hurried to the lawyer's office, where I asked if I could see the copy of the Welmingham marriage register. Mr Wansborough was a pleasant man and agreed to show me the copy. In fact, he was quite amused. No one had asked to see it since his father (now dead) had locked it away in the office more than twenty years before.

As I opened the register, my hands trembled. I turned the pages to the year and month. I found the names I remembered just before, and just after, the marriage of Sir Percival's parents. And between these entries, at the bottom of the page . . .?

Nothing! The marriage of Sir Felix Glyde and Cecilia Elster was not there! I looked again, to be sure. No, nothing. Not a doubt about it. Sir Percival must have seen the space in the Welmingham register and written in the marriage himself.

I had never once suspected this. He was not Sir Percival Glyde at all! His parents had not been married, so he had no right to the inheritance of Blackwater Park, no right to the rank of Baronet, no right even to the name of Glyde! This was his secret – and it was now mine to use against him!

The copy of the register would be safe enough in the lawyer's office, but I decided to go back to Welmingham and make a copy of the false record from the church register. It was dark now and I ran all the way to the church clerk's house. I knocked on his door, but when he appeared, he looked suspicious and confused.

'Where are the keys?' he asked. 'Have you taken them?'

'What keys do you mean?' I said. 'I've just this minute arrived from Knowlesbury.'

'The keys of the vestry,' he said. 'The keys are gone! Someone's broken in and taken the keys.'

'Get a light,' I said, 'and let's go to the vestry. Quick!'

We ran to the church. On the path we passed a man who looked at us with frightened eyes. He seemed to be a servant of some kind. We did not stop to question him, but ran on.

As we came in sight of the vestry, I saw a high window brilliantly lit from within. There was a strange smell on the night air, a sound of cracking wood, and the light grew brighter and brighter. I ran to the door and put my hand on it. The vestry was on fire!

I heard the key working violently in the lock – I heard a man's voice behind the door, raised in terror, screaming for help.

'Oh, my God!' said the servant, who had followed us, 'it's Sir Percival!'

'God help him!' said the clerk. 'He's damaged the lock.'

❖ ❖ ❖

At that moment I forget the man's crimes and see only the horror of his situation. Several people are now running towards the church and I call to them to help me break down the door. We look desperately for something to use, and at last someone finds a long heavy piece of wood.

By now the flames are shooting up out of the window, and the screams have stopped. We get the wood into position and run at the door with it. Again, and again! At last the door crashes down, but a wave of heat hits our faces and drives us back – and in the room we see nothing but a sheet of living fire.

✧ ✧ ✧

The church itself was saved as the fire engine arrived soon afterwards and managed to put out the fire before it spread. They carried out the body of Sir Percival Glyde and laid it on the wet ground. I looked down on his dead face and this was how, for the first and last time, I saw him.

'God help him! He's damaged the lock.'

He must have heard that I was free and on my way back to Welmingham, so he hurried to the church, stealing the keys and locking himself in to prevent anyone coming in and finding him. All he could do was tear the page out of the register and destroy it. If the false record no longer existed, I could produce no evidence to threaten him with. He must have dropped his lamp by accident, which started the fire. Then in his urgency to get out, the lock had become damaged and the key unmoveable.

I could not leave the town. There would be a legal enquiry into the accident the next day, which I had to attend, and in any case I had to report back to the police station in Knowlesbury. I returned to the hotel and wrote to Marian, telling her everything that had happened and warning her to keep the news from Laura for the moment. With Sir Percival's death, my hopes of establishing Laura's identity had also died, and I could see no way forward at present.

The next day an envelope with my name on was delivered to the hotel. The letter inside was neither dated nor signed, but before I had read the first sentence, I knew who had written it – Mrs Catherick.

Sir – I thought you were my enemy. Now that he is dead, because of you, I consider you my friend. To thank you for what you have done, I will now tell you the things you wanted to know about my private life.

Twenty-three years ago I was a beautiful young woman living in Welmingham, married to a fool of a husband. I also knew a gentleman – I shall not call him by his name. Why should I? It was not his own. I was born with expensive tastes. This man gave me expensive presents. Naturally he wanted something in return – all men do. And what did he want? Just a little thing. The key to the church vestry, when my husband's back was turned. I liked my presents, so I got him the key. I watched him in the vestry without his knowing, and saw what he was doing. I did not know then how serious a crime it was. I said I would not tell anyone about the marriage he had added to the register if he told me about his private life. He agreed – why, you will see in a moment.

He said that he only found out that his parents were not married after his mother's death. His father confessed to it and promised to do what he could for his son. But he died having done nothing. The son came to England and took possession of the property. There was no one to say he could not. In fact, the right person to claim the property was a distant relation away at sea. However, to borrow money on the property, he needed a certificate of his parents' marriage. This was a problem – a problem which brought him to Welmingham.

As his parents had mostly lived abroad and had had no social life in England, who was to say (the priest being dead) that a private marriage had not taken place at Welmingham church? His plan was to tear out a page from the marriage register in the year before his birth and destroy it. Then he would tell his lawyers in London to get the necessary certificate, innocently referring them to the date on the page that was gone. At least no one could say that his parents were *not* married.

However, when he saw there was a small space at the bottom of the page in the right year, he changed his plan and took the opportunity to write in the marriage himself. It took him some time, though, to practise the handwriting and to mix the right colour of ink, so that it looked the same.

After my husband caught me talking secretly to him and after their fight together, I asked my fine gentleman to clear my name and to say there had been nothing between us. But he refused. He wanted everyone to believe something false, so that they would never suspect the truth. He then told me that the punishment for his crime, and anyone who helped him, was life in prison. He frightened me! If I spoke out, I was just as lost as he was. He then agreed to make me a yearly payment if I said nothing and stayed in Welmingham, where he could always find me and where there was no danger of my making friends and talking. This was hard, but I accepted.

Many years later, when my daughter was with me at home, I received a letter from him which made me very angry. I lost control of myself and said, in her presence, that 'I could destroy him if I let out his secret'. Then one day he came to our house and called her a fool. Immediately she shouted, 'Ask for my pardon, now, or I'll let out your secret and destroy your life.' My own words! He went white. Then he swore at us. It ended, as you know, by his shutting her up in an asylum. I tried to tell him she knew nothing. But he did not believe me. My daughter knew that she had frightened him and that he was responsible for shutting her up because he believed she knew his secret. That's why she hated him. But she never to her dying day knew what his secret actually was.

I will end by saying that you insult me if you think my husband was not my daughter's father. Please do not ask further questions about that. To protect myself, I mention no names in this letter, nor do I sign it.

13

The threat

Mrs Catherick's extraordinary and shameless letter filled me with disgust. My interest in Sir Percival Glyde's crime was now at an end, but I decided to keep the letter in case it might help me find out who Anne's father really was.

Later in the morning I went to the legal enquiry into Sir Percival's death. I was only asked to say what had happened. I was not asked how I thought the keys had been taken, how the fire had been caused, or why Sir Percival had gone into the vestry. As no one could explain any of these things, the verdict at the end of the enquiry was 'death by accident'.

Afterwards, a gentleman who was also at the enquiry walked back to the hotel with me. He had heard from Sir Percival's lawyer that a distant relation abroad would now inherit Blackwater Park. This was obviously the person who should have inherited it twenty-three years before. If I made Sir Percival's crime public, it would be to no one's advantage now. If I kept the secret, the true character of the man who had cheated Laura into marrying him would remain hidden. And for her sake, I wished to keep it hidden.

I still could not leave Hampshire, as I had to report to the police station in Knowlesbury the next day. I spent another night at the hotel and in the morning went to the post office to collect the letter from Marian. As promised, we had written to each other every day, and Marian's letters had been full of cheerful news. This morning's letter was short, and terrified me.

Come back as soon as you can. We have had to move. Come to Gower's Walk, Fulham (number five). I will look out for you. Don't be alarmed about us, we are both safe and well. But come back – Marian

What had happened? What dreadful thing had Count Fosco done while I was away? In spite of my anxiety, I had to wait. I paid my bill at the hotel and took a cab to Knowlesbury.

At the police station, as I expected, no one appeared to

continue the action against me and I was allowed to go. Half an hour later I was on the train back to London.

I got to Gower's Walk in Fulham at about nine o'clock. Both Laura and Marian came to the door to let me in. Laura was much brighter and happier, full of plans for the future and for her drawing and painting. Marian's face was tired and anxious. I could see that she had spared Laura the knowledge of the terrible death in Welmingham and the true reason for moving to new lodgings. When Laura had left us and we could speak freely, I tried to give some expression to my feelings and told Marian how much I admired her for the courage and love she had shown.

She was too generous to listen to me, and turned the conversation to my worries.

'I'm so sorry for my letter – it must have alarmed you.'

'Yes, it did,' I admitted. 'Was I right in thinking that you moved because of a threat by Count Fosco?'

'Perfectly right,' she said. 'I saw him yesterday, and worse than that, Walter – I spoke to him.'

'Spoke to him? Did he come to the house?'

'He did. Yesterday, when I was passing the window, I saw him in the street. Then there was a knock on the door. I rushed out and there he was, dressed in black, with his smooth face and his deadly smile. I closed the door behind me so that Laura would not see or hear him.'

'What did he say?' I asked anxiously.

'He greeted me, then repeated the warning in his letter to me. He said he had not been able to prevent Sir Percival's violence towards you, and he had found out our address in order to protect his own interests. You were followed, Walter, on your return home after your first journey to Hampshire. He used this information only when he heard of Sir Percival's death, because he believed you would act against him next.'

'And he was right,' I said. 'What did he say about me?'

'He was very cool, very polite, and very threatening,' said Marian. 'He said, "Warn Mr Hartright! He has an intelligent and powerful man to deal with. Let him be content with what he has got. Say to him, if he attacks me, I will use all my power to destroy him. There is nothing I will not do. Dear lady, good

'There was the Count, with his smooth face and his deadly smile.'

morning." Then he just looked at me with his cold grey eyes, and walked away.

'I ran back inside, and told Laura we had to move. We needed a quieter neighbourhood with better air for the sake of her health. I said you'd wanted us to do that, and why didn't we do it now to surprise you when you got back. She liked that idea, and was quite happy to move. I found these lodgings through an old school friend. I did the right thing, didn't I, Walter?'

I answered her warmly and gratefully, as I really felt.

But the anxious look remained on her face, and I saw in her eyes her continuing fear of the Count's cleverness and energy.

'What do you think of his message, Walter? What do you plan to do next?'

'I decided weeks ago that Laura will be received in her uncle's house again,' I answered. 'And my decision remains the same. Count Fosco will answer for his crime to ME.'

Marian's eyes lit up. She said nothing, but I could see how strongly she supported this plan.

'I know the risks are great,' I said, 'but it must be done. I'm not foolish enough to try this before I'm well prepared. I can wait. Let him think his message has produced its effect. He will start to feel safe. Also, my position towards you and Laura ought to be a stronger one than it is now.'

'How can it be stronger?' she asked, surprised.

'Marian, I would like you to say to Laura, gently, that her husband is dead.'

'Oh, Walter, so soon? You have a reason for this, don't you?'

'Yes. I cannot speak to Laura yet. But one day, not too distant, I want to tell her that I love her.'

Marian looked at me for a time, then gave a sad, gentle smile. 'Yes, I understand. I think I owe it to her and to you, Walter, to tell her of her husband's death.'

The next day Laura knew that death had released her from her marriage, and her husband's name was never mentioned among us again.

❖ ❖ ❖

Our life returned to its usual pattern, but I did not forget the Count. I discovered that he had rented his house in St John's Wood for another six months, so I was fairly sure he would still be in London, within my reach, when the time came to act.

We finally solved the puzzle of who Anne Catherick's father was. When I went again to see Mrs Clements and to tell her about Anne's death, she remembered where Mrs Catherick had worked as a servant. Her employer had been a Mr Donthorne.

We wrote to Mr Donthorne, who replied with some very interesting information. Philip Fairlie, Laura's father, had been a great friend of his when they were young, and a frequent house guest. He was a handsome man and fond of female company. Mr Donthorne was fairly certain that Philip Fairlie had been staying at his house when Mrs Catherick was employed as a servant, in the year before Anne was born.

When Marian and I checked the dates; when we considered that Anne and Laura looked so alike; and when we took into account the fact that Laura looked very much like her father, we were in no doubt that here was the solution. Philip Fairlie was Anne's father, and so Anne was Laura's half-sister.

Now, at last, the woman in white, that strange sad shadow walking in the loneliness of the night, could rest in peace.

❖ ❖ ❖

Four months passed. Laura grew stronger in body and in mind. She was almost her old self, and when we talked, it was as we used to talk at Limmeridge. If I touched her by accident, I felt my heart beating fast, and I saw the answering colour in her face.

In April, we went for a holiday at the seaside. While we were there I told Marian that when we returned to London, I was determined to force a confession from Count Fosco – to make him tell me the real date of Laura's journey to London.

'But if I am to challenge the Count, for Laura's safety, I think I should challenge him as her husband. Do you agree, Marian?'

'With every word,' she said. 'I parted you both once. Wait here, my brother, my best and dearest friend! till Laura comes, and tells you what I have done now!'

She kissed my forehead and left the room. I waited by the window, staring out at the beach, seeing nothing, hardly able to breathe. The door opened, and Laura came in alone. When we parted at Limmeridge, she had come into the room slowly, in sorrow and hesitation. Now she ran to me, with the light of happiness shining in her face. She put her arms around me, and her sweet lips came to meet mine.

'My darling!' she whispered, 'may we say we love each other now? Oh, I am so happy at last!'

Ten days later we were even happier. We were married.

14

The confession

A fortnight later, we returned to London, and I began to prepare for my battle with the Count. It was now early May and the rental agreement for his house ended in June. In my new happiness with Laura (to whom we never mentioned the Count's name), I was sometimes tempted to change my mind and to leave things as they were. But she still had dreams, terrible dreams that made her cry out in her sleep, and I knew I had to go on.

First, I tried to find out more about the Count. Marian told me that he had not been back to Italy for many years. Had he been obliged to leave Italy for political reasons, I wondered? But Marian also said that at Blackwater Park he had received official-looking letters with Italian stamps on, which would seem to contradict this idea. Perhaps he was a spy, I thought. That might explain why he had stayed in England so long after the successful completion of his plot. Who could I ask who might know something? Another Italian, perhaps – and I suddenly thought of my old friend, Professor Pesca.

Before I did that, I decided to have a look at the Count, as up to this time I had never once set eyes on him. So one morning I went to Forest Road, St John's Wood, and waited near his house. Eventually, he came out and I followed behind him as he walked towards the centre of London. Marian had prepared me for his enormous size and fashionable clothes, but not for the horrible freshness and cheerfulness and energy of the man.

Near Oxford Street he stopped to read a sign announcing an opera, and then went into the opera ticket office, which was nearby. I went over to read the sign. The opera was being performed that evening, and it seemed likely that the Count would be in the audience.

If I invite Pesca to the opera, I thought, I can point the Count out to him and find out if he knows him. So I bought two tickets myself, sent Pesca a note, and that evening called to take him with me to the opera.

The music had already started when we went in, and all the seats were filled. However, there was room to stand at the sides. I looked around and saw the Count sitting in a seat half-way down, so I placed myself exactly on a line with him, with Pesca standing at my side. When the first part finished, the audience, including the Count, rose to look about them.

When the Count was looking in our direction, I nudged Pesca with my elbow. 'You see that tall fat man? Do you know him?'

'No,' said Pesca. 'Is he famous? Why do you point him out?'

'Because I have a reason for wanting to know more about him. He's an Italian, and his name is Count Fosco. Do you know that name? Look – stand on this step so that you can see him better.'

A slim, fair-haired man, with a scar on his left cheek, was standing near us. I saw him look at Pesca, and then follow the direction of his eyes to the Count. Pesca repeated that he did not know him, and as he spoke, the Count looked our way again.

The eyes of the two Italians met.

In that second I was suddenly convinced that, while Pesca may not have known the Count, the Count certainly knew Pesca!

Not only knew him, but – more surprising still – *feared* him as well. The Count's face had frozen into a dreadful stillness, the cheeks as pale as death, the cold grey eyes staring in terror.

Nearby, the man with the scar also seemed to be watching with interest the effect that Pesca had had on the Count.

'How the fat man stares!' Pesca said, looking round at me. 'But I've never seen him before in my life.'

As Pesca looked away, the Count turned, moving quickly towards the back of the theatre, where the crowd was thickest. I caught Pesca's arm and, to his great surprise, hurried him with me after the Count. The slim man with the scar had apparently also decided to leave, and was already ahead of us. By the time Pesca and I reached the entrance, neither the Count nor the slim man was in sight.

'Pesca,' I said urgently, 'I must speak to you in private. May we go to your lodgings to talk?'

'What on earth is the matter?' cried Pesca.

I hurried him on without answering. The way the Count had left the theatre, his extraordinary anxiety to avoid Pesca, made me fear that he might go even further – and out of my reach.

In Pesca's lodgings, I explained everything as fast as I could, while Pesca stared at me in great confusion and amazement.

'*He* knows *you* – he's afraid of you. He left the theatre to escape you,' I said. 'There must be a reason, Pesca! Think of your own life before you came to England. You left Italy for political reasons. I don't ask what they were. But could that man's terror be connected with your past in some way?'

To my inexpressible surprise, these harmless words seemed to terrify Pesca. His face went white and he started to tremble.

'Walter!' he whispered. 'You don't know what you ask.'

I stared at him. 'Pesca, forgive me. I didn't mean to cause you pain. I spoke only because of what my wife has suffered from that man's cruel actions. You must forgive me.'

I rose to go. He stopped me before I reached the door.

'Wait,' he said. 'You saved my life once. You have a right to hear from me what you want to know, even though I could be killed for it. I only ask that, if you find the connection between my past and that man Fosco, you do not tell me.'

Then, his face still pale as the memories of the past crowded in on him, he told me the story.

'In my youth I belonged – and still belong – to a secret political society. Let's call it the Brotherhood, I can't tell you its real name. But I took too many risks and did something which put other members in danger. So I was ordered to go and live in England and to wait. I went – I have waited – I still wait. I could be called away tomorrow, or in ten years. I cannot know.

'The purpose of the Brotherhood is to fight for the rights of the people. There is a president in Italy, and presidents abroad. Each of these has his secretary. The presidents and secretaries know the members, but members don't know each other, until it's considered necessary. Every member of the Brotherhood is identified by a small round mark burnt into the skin, high up on the inside of their left arm.'

He rolled up his sleeve and showed me his own mark.

'If anyone betrays the Brotherhood,' he went on, 'he is a dead man. Another member, a distant stranger or a neighbour, will be ordered to kill him. No one can leave the society – ever.'

Pesca paused, then continued. 'In Italy I was chosen to be secretary. The members at that time were brought face to face with the president, and were also brought face to face with *me*. You understand me – I see it in your face. But tell me nothing, I beg you! Let me stay free of a responsibility which horrifies me.

'I do not know the man at the opera,' he said finally. 'If he knows *me*, he is so changed, or disguised, that I do not know *him*. Leave me now, Walter. I have said enough.'

'I thank you with all my heart, Pesca,' I said. 'You will never, never regret the trust you have placed in me.'

Walking home, my heart beat with excitement. Here at last, surely, was my weapon against the Count! I was convinced he was a member of the Brotherhood, had betrayed it, and believed that he had been recognized tonight. His life was now in danger. What else could explain his extreme terror at seeing Pesca?

And what would he do next? Leave London as fast as he could. If I went to his house and tried to stop him, he would not hesitate to kill me. To protect myself, I had to make *his* safety depend on *mine*. I hurried home and wrote this letter to Pesca:

The man at the opera, Fosco, is a member of your society and has betrayed it. Go instantly to his house at 5 Forest Road, St John's Wood. I am already dead. Use your power against him without delay.

I signed and dated the letter, and wrote on the envelope: *Keep until nine o'clock tomorrow morning. If you do not hear from me before then, open the envelope and read the contents.*

I then found a messenger, told him to deliver the letter and bring back a note from Professor Pesca to say he had received it. Twenty minutes later I had the note, and as I was leaving, Marian came to the door, looking anxious.

'It's tonight, isn't it?' she said. 'You're going to the Count.'

'Yes, it's the last chance, and the best.'

'Oh, Walter, not alone! Let me go with you. Don't go alone!'

'No, Marian. You must stay here and guard Laura for me. Then I will be easy in my mind when I face the Count.'

✧ ✧ ✧

As I approached the Count's house, I passed the man with the scar on his cheek, whom I had noticed earlier at the opera. What was he doing here, I wondered?

I sent in my card, and I still do not know why the Count let me into his house at half past eleven at night. Was he just curious to see me? He would not have known that I was at the opera with Pesca, and I suppose he thought he had nothing to fear from me.

He was still in his evening suit, and there was a travelling case on the floor, with books, papers, and clothes all around him. My guess had been right.

'You come here on business, Mr Hartright?' he said, looking at me with curiosity. 'I cannot think what that might be.'

'You are obviously preparing for a journey,' I said. 'That is my business. I know why you are leaving London.'

'So you know why I am leaving London?' He went over to a table and opened a drawer. 'Tell me the reason, if you please.'

'I can *show* you the reason,' I said. 'Roll up the sleeve on your left arm, and you will see it.'

His cold grey eyes stared into mine. There was a long heartbeat of silence. I was as certain as if I had seen it that he had a gun hidden in the drawer, and that my life hung by a thread.

'Wait a little,' I said. 'Before you act, I advise you to read this note.' Moving slowly and carefully, I passed him Pesca's note.

He read the lines aloud.

Your letter is received. If I don't hear from you before nine o'clock, I will open the envelope when the clock strikes.

Another man might have needed an explanation, but not the Count. His expression changed, and he closed the drawer.

'You are cleverer than I thought,' he said. 'I cannot leave before nine as I have to wait for a passport to be delivered. Your information may be true or may be false – where did you get it?'

'I refuse to tell you.'

'And that unsigned note you showed me – who wrote it?'

'A man whom you have every reason to fear.'

A pause. 'What do you want of me, Mr Hartright? Is it to do with a lady, perhaps?'

'Yes, my wife,' I answered.

He looked at me in real amazement, and I saw at once that he no longer considered me a dangerous man. He folded his arms and listened to me with a cold smile.

'You are guilty of a wicked crime,' I went on. 'But you can keep the money. All I want is a signed confession of the plot and a proof of the date my wife travelled to London.'

'Good!' he said. 'Those are your conditions; here are mine. One, Madame Fosco and I leave the house when we please and you do not try to stop us. Two, you wait here until my agent comes early tomorrow morning and you give him an order to get back your letter unopened. You then allow us half an hour to leave the house. Three, you agree to fight me at a place to be arranged later abroad. Do you accept my conditions – yes or no?'

His quick decision, his cleverness and force of character amazed me. For a second I hesitated. Should I let him escape? Yes, the evidence I needed to prove Laura's identity was far more important than revenge.

'I accept your conditions,' I said.

At once, he called for coffee and sat down to write. He wrote quickly for quite some time. Finally, he jumped up, declared that he had finished and read out his statement, which I accepted as satisfactory. He gave me the address of the company from whom he had hired the cab to collect Laura, and also gave me a letter signed by Sir Percival. It was dated 25th July, and announced the journey of Lady Glyde to London on 26th July. So there it was. On 25th July, the date of her death certificate in London, Laura was alive in Hampshire, about to make a journey the next day.

The Count then called in Madame Fosco to watch me while he slept. Early in the morning his agent arrived and I wrote a note for Pesca. An hour later, the agent returned with my unopened letter and the Count's passport.

'Remember the third condition!' the Count said as he left. 'You will hear from me, Mr Hartright.' Then he and the Countess got into the agent's cab with their bags and drove away, leaving the agent with me to make sure I did not follow.

As I watched them leave, another cab went by and I saw inside the man with the scar on his cheek. What was his business with the Count, I wondered? I had seen him too often now for it to be chance. Perhaps I had fought my own battle with the Count just in time. You cannot get a signed confession out of a dead man.

While I waited for the agreed half hour, I read the document that the Count had written for me.

STATEMENT BY ISIDOR OTTAVIO BALDASSARE FOSCO

In the summer of 1850 I arrived in England on delicate political business and stayed with my friend, Sir Percival Glyde. We both urgently needed large amounts of money. The only person who had such money was his wife, from whom not a penny could be obtained until her death. To make matters worse, my friend had other private problems. A woman called Anne Catherick was hidden in the neighbourhood, was communicating with Lady Glyde, and knew a secret which could ruin him. And if he was ruined, what would happen to our financial interests?

The first thing to do was to find Anne Catherick, who, I was told, looked very much like Lady Glyde and who had escaped from a mad-house. I had the fantastic idea of changing the names, places and lives of Lady Glyde and Anne Catherick, the one with the other. The wonderful results of this change would be the gain of £30,000 and the keeping of Sir Percival's secret.

I found Anne Catherick and persuaded her and her friend to return to London. I rented a house in St John's Wood for myself, and obtained from Mr Fairlie in Limmeridge an invitation for Lady Glyde to visit. For my plan to work, it was necessary for Lady Glyde to leave Blackwater Park alone and stay a night at my house on her way to Limmeridge. This plan was made easier by Miss Halcombe's illness. I returned to Blackwater Park, and when Miss Halcombe was out of danger, I got rid of the doctor and instructed Sir Percival to get rid of the servants.

Next, we sent Mrs Michelson away for a few days, and one night Madame Fosco, Mrs Rubelle and I moved the sleeping Miss Halcombe to an unused part of the house. I left for London in the morning with my wife, leaving Sir Percival to persuade Lady Glyde that her sister had gone to Limmeridge and that she should follow her, breaking her journey in London at my house.

On 24th July, with my wife's help, I got hold of Anne Catherick, and took her to my house as Lady Glyde. However, when she saw no one she recognized, she screamed with fear and, to my horror, the shock to her weak heart caused her to collapse. By the end of the following day, she was dead. Dead on the 25th, and Lady Glyde was not due to arrive in London till the 26th!

It was too late to change the plan. I remained calm and carried on. On the 26th, leaving the false Lady Glyde dead in my house, I collected the true Lady Glyde from the railway station and took her to Mrs Rubelle's house. The two medical men I had hired (shall we say) were easily persuaded to certify the confused and frightened Lady Glyde as mentally ill. Then I gave her a drug and had Mrs Rubelle dress her in Anne Catherick's clothes. The next day, the 27th, she was delivered to the asylum, where she was received with great surprise, but without suspicion. The false Lady Glyde was buried at Limmeridge. I attended the funeral with suitable expressions of deep sympathy.

One final question remains. If Anne Catherick had not died when she did, what would I have done? I would, of course, have given her a happy release from the prison of life.

15

The proof

When the half hour had passed, I returned home. After a brief explanation to Laura and Marian, I hurried back to St John's Wood to find the cab-driver whom the Count had hired to collect Laura at the station. He wrote me a statement, which he and a witness signed, saying that on 26th July 1850 he had driven a Count Fosco to the railway station where they had collected a Lady Glyde. He remembered Lady Glyde's name, he said, from the labels on her luggage.

Then I went to Mr Kyrle's office and presented him with the proof of Laura's identity – the letter from Sir Percival, the statement by the cab-driver, the confession by the Count, and the death certificate. Amazed, he congratulated me, and agreed to accompany us to Limmeridge the next day, where I intended to have Laura publicly received and recognized.

Early the next morning Laura, Marian, Mr Kyrle and I took the train to Limmeridge. Laura and Marian stayed at first in a hotel while Mr Kyrle and I went to the house to deal with Mr

'On the 27th July, Lady Glyde was delivered to the asylum.'

Fairlie. He complained like a child, saying how was he to know his niece was alive when he was told she was dead? Between us, the lawyer and I made him sign letters calling all those who had attended the false funeral to come to the house the next day.

As I led Laura into her childhood home the following morning, there was a murmur of surprise and interest from the waiting crowd of villagers and neighbours. The business was soon done. I read out the story of the plot against Laura, and Mr Kyrle announced that everything I had said was proved by the strongest evidence. I put my arm around Laura, raised her up, and called to the crowd:

'Are you all agreed that this is the Laura Fairlie you knew?'

'There she is, alive and well – God bless her!' It was an old man at the back of the room who began it, and in an instant everybody was shouting and cheering together.

Later, in the churchyard, we watched a stone worker remove Laura's name from the gravestone. In its place he put this:

ANNE CATHERICK

25TH JULY 1850

We returned to London the following day, happy in the thought that the long struggle was now over.

✦ ✦ ✦

Several days later Pesca came to see me, and asked for a quiet word in my ear. He had just returned from Paris.

'I have news for you, my friend,' he said. 'You need not worry any more about the man at the opera. His body was found in the river Seine yesterday and now lies in the morgue in Paris. He was killed by knife wounds to the heart.'

'Count Fosco is dead?' I said, amazed. 'Are you sure?'

'I saw the body with my own eyes. He was wearing a French workman's clothes, and had a different name, of course, but he was the fat man we saw at the opera that night. No question.'

'But how do you know this?' I asked.

Pesca hesitated. 'A man brought me some information,' he said. 'I had to see the body, and send a report about it.'

'A man,' I said. 'What kind of man?'

'A stranger,' said Pesca. 'I didn't know him. A man with a scar on his left cheek.' He saw the understanding in my face, and held up his hand. 'No more questions, my friend. Please!'

We never spoke about it again, but I think Pesca was telling me that the Brotherhood had taken their revenge. And so Count Fosco, that extraordinary, evil man, passed from this world.

✦ ✦ ✦

The following year our first child was born – a son. Six months later my newspaper sent me to Ireland and, when I returned, I found a note from my wife saying she and Marian and little Walter had gone to Limmeridge House. She begged me to follow as soon as possible. Very surprised, I caught the next train. When I got there, Marian and Laura told me Mr Fairlie was dead and that Mr Kyrle had advised them to go to Limmeridge House.

Laura came close to me and I half realized some great change was happening in our lives.

'Do you know who this is, Walter?' Marian asked, holding up my little son, with tears of happiness in her eyes. 'This is the boy who will one day inherit Limmeridge House.'

So she spoke. In writing those last words, I have written everything. Marian was the good friend of our lives – let Marian end our story.

∾

GLOSSARY

asylum a hospital where people who are mentally ill can be cared for

bail an amount of money that someone agrees to pay if a person accused of a crime does not appear for trial

Baronet a nobleman who has the title 'Sir' and can pass the title on to his son when he dies

bless (*v*) to ask God to protect somebody

cab (here) a horse and carriage available for public hire

capital a large amount of money that is owned by someone

cloak a loose kind of coat that fastens at the neck and has no sleeves

Count the title of a nobleman in some European countries

Countess the title of the wife of a count

feature a part of someone's face, such as the nose, eyes, etc.

footprint a mark left on the ground by someone's foot or shoe

footsteps the sound made by feet walking or running

gentleman (in this story) a man from a high social class, well-educated and usually wealthy (i.e. not a servant or a workman)

gloomy dark, miserable; sad and without hope

governess a woman employed to teach the children of a rich family in their home

guardian someone who is legally responsible for a young person whose parents are dead

hood a kind of hat, attached to a coat or cloak, which covers the top and back of the head

housekeeper a person employed to manage and look after someone else's house

identity who a person is

Lady a title used by the wife or daughter of a nobleman

loan an amount of money that a person or bank lends to
    someone

lodgings a room in someone's house that you rent to live in

magistrate a judge who deals with smaller crimes in local courts

mental connected with the health of the mind

morgue a building where dead bodies are kept before burial

nerves the long thin threads in the body that carry messages
    between the brain and other parts of the body

nobleman a man who has a title and who is from a very old
    family of high social rank

nudge to give someone a gentle push to get their attention

opera a play in which most of the words are sung to music

post-bag (in former times) a bag in which all the letters of the
    house are collected to be taken to the post

rank the position that somebody has in society

register (*n*) an official record of births, marriages, and deaths

rustle (*v*) to make a sound like papers, leaves, etc. rubbing
    together

scar a mark left on the skin after a wound has healed

shiver (*v*) to tremble from cold, or with fear, excitement, etc.

sketch (*v & n*) to make a quick, simple drawing of something

typhus a serious infectious disease that causes fever, headaches,
    and often death

veil a covering of thin material worn by women to hide the face

verandah a platform with a roof, built onto the side of a house
    on the ground floor

vestry a room in a church where things like church records and
    the priest's clothes are kept

The Woman in White

ACTIVITIES

ACTIVITIES

Before Reading

1   Read the story introduction on the first page of the book, and
the back cover. What kind of secret, do you think, could bring 'ruin
and shame' to a man in nineteenth-century England? Put these
possibilities in order of likelihood, and add any ideas of your own.

- living beyond his income and never paying his debts
- stealing money from a rich relative
- spending all his wife's inherited money
- inheriting money and property not rightfully his
- getting a woman pregnant and not marrying her
- having unmarried parents
- having two wives
- keeping a mistress
- abandoning his wife and leaving her penniless
- beating his wife
- beating his servants
- cheating at cards

2   What can you predict about this kind of story? Choose words of
your own to complete this passage (one word for each gap).

In thrillers of this kind, the mystery is usually _____ in the end,
though often in an _____ way. The good characters have to
_____ against the forces of evil, but they learn from their _____,
and usually live _____ ever after. The wicked characters, who are
sometimes more _____ than the good ones, _____ succeed in
their aims and are often _____ by death or imprisonment.

ACTIVITIES

While Reading

Read Part One (Chapters 1 to 3), and complete this passage with the names of people and places given below.

Laura / Marian / Walter / Anne Catherick / Sir Percival (Glyde) / woman in white / Baronet / Fairlie / Limmeridge House / Hampshire / London

_____ came to _____ as a drawing teacher to _____ and _____, who were half-sisters. _____'s family name was _____ – a name mentioned by the strange _____ that _____ had met in _____. She had told him that she came from _____ but had once been very happy at _____. He told _____ this story, and she discovered from old letters of her mother's that the _____ was probably _____.

A few months later _____ advised _____ to leave, as she had realized he was in love with _____, who was already promised in marriage to _____, a _____ from _____. But before _____ left, an unsigned letter came for _____, warning her not to marry _____, and _____ believed the letter had been sent by _____, whom he found that evening, cleaning Mrs _____'s grave in the churchyard.

Before you read Part Two, which is told by Marian Halcombe, can you guess how the story develops? Think about these questions.

1 How does Marian feel about Walter Hartright?
2 How does Laura react to the arrival of Sir Percival?
3 Does Sir Percival's explanation about Anne Catherick's letter satisfy Marian and Mr Gilmore?
4 How does Walter try to get over his heartbreak?

Read Part Two (Chapters 4 to 8). Here are some untrue sentences about these chapters. Rewrite them with the correct information.

1 Laura told Sir Percival that she loved Walter Hartright, and Sir Percival offered to release her from the engagement.

2 The marriage agreement was very much to Laura's advantage.

3 Sir Percival tried to get hold of Laura's money by copying her signature without her knowledge.

4 Count Fosco knew that Marian had written to Mr Kyrle because he heard her talking to Laura about it.

5 When Laura met Anne Catherick at the lake, Anne said nothing about Sir Percival.

6 Sir Percival threatened to lock Laura up until she gave him the money he needed.

7 While hiding behind a desk in the library, Marian heard Count Fosco and Sir Percival discussing how Anne Catherick's death would solve the problem of their debt.

8 Laura went to the Count's house in London although she knew Marian was still at Blackwater Park.

Before you read Part Three, which is told by Walter Hartright, what do you think might happen next? Choose some of these possibilities, or think of your own.

1 Walter Hartright returns to England and he . . .

    a) investigates Laura's death.   c) has Count Fosco arrested.

    b) discovers Sir Percival's   d) eventually marries
       secret.   Marian.

2 Sir Percival . . .

    a) inherits his wife's money.   c) dies in an accident.

    b) quarrels with Count Fosco.   d) is killed by Walter.

Read Part Three, up to the end of Chapter 13 on page 92. Who said or wrote these words, and to whom? Who or what were they talking about?

1 'Oh God, help him! Please, please help him, God!'
2 'We just ran into each other's arms, unable to say a word.'
3 'I don't recognize this woman. Remove her from my house before I call on the law to protect me.'
4 'If he crosses my path, he is a lost man.'
5 'It's the one weak point in their plot.'
6 'I agreed to go with this lady to make the arrangement, leaving Anne alone in our lodgings. But it was a wicked plot, sir.'
7 'Have you come to tell me that she is dead?'
8 'From a great family! Yes, indeed! Especially from his mother's side.'
9 'God help him! He's damaged the lock.'
10 'He wanted everyone to believe something false, so that they would never suspect the truth.'
11 'Come back as soon as you can. We have had to move.'
12 'I can wait. Let him think his message has produced its effect.'
13 'Wait here, my brother, my best and dearest friend!'
14 'Oh, I am so happy at last!'

Before you read Chapters 14 and 15 (*The confession* and *The proof*), can you guess how the story ends?

1 How does Professor Pesca come into the end of the story?
2 How does Walter force the Count to confess to the plot?
3 Does the Count return any of Laura's money?
4 How does Mr Fairlie react to proof of Laura's identity?
5 What happens when Mr Fairlie dies?

ACTIVITIES

After Reading

1 **Perhaps this is what some of the characters in the story were thinking. Which characters are they, who or what are they thinking about, and what is happening at this point in the story?**

1 'I must tear the page out and destroy it. It's my only chance. Then there'll be no evidence, no proof. Ah, here it is! Now, I need more light . . . quick, move the lamp closer – Oh no! NO!'

2 'He asks if I remember him, but I don't think I do. Do I? Have I seen him before? Wait . . . His face . . . Yes, yes, I remember now! He's that kind man I met on Hampstead Heath . . .'

3 'I don't know what Marian thinks she's doing – banging doors, bringing that madwoman in here, saying I must recognize her as my niece! I think Marian must be going mad herself . . .'

4 'There's a little hole in the sand down there, just by the boat-house wall. I can see something in it – it looks like paper . . . Yes, it's a note! She's left me a note! Quick, what does it say?'

5 'That must be her, in the summer-house. She's coming out to greet us. What a lovely face! And those eyes – so clear, so blue!'

6 'It's nearly seven o'clock in the morning. He's been gone all night! Whatever can have happened? What shall I do, what shall I do? No, I must stay here, and guard Laura, as he told me . . .'

7 'The man is an idiot! What does he hope to gain by shouting at her like that? She'll never sign it now. And her sister is getting suspicious. I must put a stop to this nonsense at once . . .'

2 **Three days after Marian fell ill with typhus at Blackwater Park, Count Fosco explained his plan to Sir Percival. Complete the Count's side of the conversation. Use as many words as you like.**

COUNT FOSCO: I have it, Percival – the perfect plan! Within a few weeks you will be a widower, and able to pay all your debts!

SIR PERCIVAL: If you're talking about my wife's death, forget it!

COUNT FOSCO: Ah, but suppose _____

SIR PERCIVAL: Another woman? What are you talking about?

COUNT FOSCO: _____

SIR PERCIVAL: Yes, they do look very similar. But how the devil are you going to get them to change places?

COUNT FOSCO: _____

SIR PERCIVAL: But you haven't got a house in London. And why should my wife want to go to Limmeridge?

COUNT FOSCO: _____

SIR PERCIVAL: Ah, Marian . . . yes, I see. So, you get Lady Glyde to London. What happens then?

COUNT FOSCO: _____

SIR PERCIVAL: But won't the asylum release her when she tells them who she really is?

COUNT FOSCO: _____

SIR PERCIVAL: Mm, I hope you're right. And Anne Catherick? You say you persuaded this friend of hers, Mrs Clements, when you met her at the lake, to take her back to London?

COUNT FOSCO: _____

SIR PERCIVAL: She has heart disease? How do you know that?

COUNT FOSCO: _____

SIR PERCIVAL: Yes, yes, very clever. But suppose her heart disease is not very advanced – suppose she doesn't die, Fosco? What then?

COUNT FOSCO: _____

3 Here are some extracts from letters described or referred to in the
text. Who is writing to whom? Fill in the names, and complete the
extracts with one suitable word for each gap.

1 _____ to _____
   . . . you will be glad _____ know Anne Catherick has _____
   found and taken back _____ the asylum. She is _____ very
   disturbed mentally, and _____ now claiming she is _____
   Anne Catherick at all, _____ Lady Glyde, your niece _____
   died recently. You should _____ aware of this, in _____ she
   escapes again and _____ to annoy you or _____ members of
   Lady Glyde's _____ . . .

2 _____ to _____
   . . . as I was very _____ yesterday to receive a _____ addressed
   to me – I _____ your handwriting on the _____ – which
   contained nothing but _____ plain piece of paper _____ a
   word on it. _____ do hope there is _____ wrong, and I look
   _____ to hearing from you _____ in the very near _____ . . .

3 _____ to _____
   . . . I write to you _____ some very sad news _____ my niece.
   She was _____ seriously ill when she _____ at our house in
   _____, and she died the _____ day, very suddenly. It _____
   been a great shock _____ everybody. Please break the _____ as
   gently as you _____ to her sister, who _____ still be very weak
   _____ her illness . . .

4 _____ to _____
   . . . I fear the situation _____ her and Sir Percival _____
   getting worse day by _____. Laura really needs to _____ from
   him, and you _____ write to invite her _____ Limmeridge. It is
   very _____ that you do this _____ delay, as I am _____

something terrible will happen _____ Laura does not leave
_____ soon . . .

5 _____ to _____

Blackwater Park, _____ July.
Everything has gone _____ to plan. Lady Glyde _____ on
following her sister _____ her uncle's house, and _____ be
taking the train _____ London tomorrow, on the _____ July.
I told her _____ will meet her at _____ station, and that she
_____ stay at your house _____ the night.

Now read the completed extracts again. Put the letters in the order
they were written in the story, and explain the circumstances
surrounding each one. Which letter is the most important one for
the plot, and why?

4 What do you think about the way these people behaved? Was it
foolish, cowardly, irresponsible, wicked, criminal? Did some of them
have excuses for behaving in this way? Discuss your ideas.

- Mrs Catherick's treatment of her daughter Anne.
- Sir Percival's false entry in the marriage register, so that he
  could inherit his father's title and property.
- Anne Catherick's unsigned letter to Laura about Sir Percival.
- Marian telling Walter he must leave Limmeridge, because he
  had fallen in love with Laura.
- Sir Percival locking up Anne Catherick in an asylum.
- Laura telling Sir Percival that she loved another man.
- Madame Fosco helping her husband by stealing people's letters.
- Count Fosco and Sir Percival changing the identities of Laura
  and Anne Catherick, in order to steal Laura's money; certifying
  Laura as mentally ill, and causing Anne's early death.

ABOUT THE AUTHOR

William Wilkie Collins was born in 1824 in the Marylebone area of London, where he lived for most of his life. Although he trained as a lawyer, he never practised, preferring instead to write. His second novel, *Basil* (1852), attracted the attention of Charles Dickens, and the two became friends and remained close until Dickens's death in 1870.

Real success came with the publication in 1860 of Collins's fifth novel, *The Woman in White*, a brilliant example of the 'novels of sensation' of the time. These were a powerful mixture of guilty secrets, murder, insanity; chapters which ended on a point of high suspense; and written documents such as diary entries, telegrams, and legal papers which proved crucial to the plot. Collins followed his own advice to the novelist – 'Make them laugh, make them cry, make them wait' – and his novels, which were enormously popular, can be seen as the ancestors of modern detective stories. *The Woman in White* was followed by *No Name*, *Armadale*, and in 1868 *The Moonstone*, another famous title. He wrote many other less successful novels, and also plays, short stories, and non-fiction.

Collins's home life was complicated and unusual. He never married, but lived with a widow called Caroline Graves from 1858. In 1868 he began another relationship with Martha Rudd, who had three children by him, and Collins continued his relationships with both women until his death in 1889. His will divided his property equally between the two women; interestingly, he added a 'Laura Fairlie' clause so that his daughter could not give away her money to her husband. Unfortunately, her husband, a lawyer, found a way to get round this and made off with her money – only to die soon afterwards.

OXFORD BOOKWORMS LIBRARY

Classics • Crime & Mystery • Factfiles • Fantasy & Horror
Human Interest • Playscripts • Thriller & Adventure
True Stories • World Stories

The OXFORD BOOKWORMS LIBRARY provides enjoyable reading in English, with a wide range of classic and modern fiction, non-fiction, and plays. It includes original and adapted texts in seven carefully graded language stages, which take learners from beginner to advanced level. An overview is given on the next pages.

All Stage 1 titles are available as audio recordings, as well as over eighty other titles from Starter to Stage 6. All Starters and many titles at Stages 1 to 4 are specially recommended for younger learners. Every Bookworm is illustrated, and Starters and Factfiles have full-colour illustrations.

The OXFORD BOOKWORMS LIBRARY also offers extensive support. Each book contains an introduction to the story, notes about the author, a glossary, and activities. Additional resources include tests and worksheets, and answers for these and for the activities in the books. There is advice on running a class library, using audio recordings, and the many ways of using Oxford Bookworms in reading programmes. Resource materials are available on the website <www.oup.com/bookworms>.

The *Oxford Bookworms Collection* is a series for advanced learners. It consists of volumes of short stories by well-known authors, both classic and modern. Texts are not abridged or adapted in any way, but carefully selected to be accessible to the advanced student.

You can find details and a full list of titles in the *Oxford Bookworms Library Catalogue* and *Oxford English Language Teaching Catalogues*, and on the website <www.oup.com/bookworms>.

THE OXFORD BOOKWORMS LIBRARY
GRADING AND SAMPLE EXTRACTS

STARTER • 250 HEADWORDS

present simple – present continuous – imperative –
can/cannot, must – *going to* (future) – simple gerunds …

Her phone is ringing – but where is it?

Sally gets out of bed and looks in her bag. No phone. She looks under the bed. No phone. Then she looks behind the door. There is her phone. Sally picks up her phone and answers it. *Sally's Phone*

STAGE 1 • 400 HEADWORDS

… past simple – coordination with *and, but, or* –
subordination with *before, after, when, because, so* …

I knew him in Persia. He was a famous builder and I worked with him there. For a time I was his friend, but not for long. When he came to Paris, I came after him – I wanted to watch him. He was a very clever, very dangerous man. *The Phantom of the Opera*

STAGE 2 • 700 HEADWORDS

… present perfect – *will* (future) – *(don't) have to, must not, could* –
comparison of adjectives – simple *if* clauses – past continuous –
tag questions – *ask/tell* + infinitive …

While I was writing these words in my diary, I decided what to do. I must try to escape. I shall try to get down the wall outside. The window is high above the ground, but I have to try. I shall take some of the gold with me – if I escape, perhaps it will be helpful later. *Dracula*

STAGE 3 • 1000 HEADWORDS

… should, may – present perfect continuous – *used to* – past perfect –
causative – relative clauses – indirect statements …

Of course, it was most important that no one should see
Colin, Mary, or Dickon entering the secret garden. So Colin
gave orders to the gardeners that they must all keep away
from that part of the garden in future. *The Secret Garden*

STAGE 4 • 1400 HEADWORDS

… past perfect continuous – passive (simple forms) –
would conditional clauses – indirect questions –
relatives with *where/when* – gerunds after prepositions/phrases …

I was glad. Now Hyde could not show his face to the world
again. If he did, every honest man in London would be proud
to report him to the police. *Dr Jekyll and Mr Hyde*

STAGE 5 • 1800 HEADWORDS

… future continuous – future perfect –
passive (modals, continuous forms) –
would have conditional clauses – modals + perfect infinitive …

If he had spoken Estella's name, I would have hit him. I was so
angry with him, and so depressed about my future, that I could
not eat the breakfast. Instead I went straight to the old house.
Great Expectations

STAGE 6 • 2500 HEADWORDS

… passive (infinitives, gerunds) – advanced modal meanings –
clauses of concession, condition

When I stepped up to the piano, I was confident. It was as if I
knew that the prodigy side of me really did exist. And when I
started to play, I was so caught up in how lovely I looked that
I didn't worry how I would sound. *The Joy Luck Club*

BOOKWORMS • THRILLER & ADVENTURE • STAGE 6

Night Without End

ALISTAIR MACLEAN

Retold by Margaret Naudi

On the Polar ice-cap, 640 kilometres north of the Arctic Circle, the deadly, icy winds can freeze a man to death in minutes. But the survivors of the crashed airliner are lucky – they are rescued by three scientists from a nearby weather station.

But why did the airliner crash in the first place? Who smashed the radio to pieces? And why does the dead pilot have a bullet hole in his back? The rescue quickly turns into a nightmare: a race through the endless Arctic night, a race against time, cold, hunger – and a killer with a gun.

BOOKWORMS • HUMAN INTEREST • STAGE 6

The Joy Luck Club

AMY TAN

Retold by Clare West

There are so many things that a mother wishes to teach her daughter. How to lose your innocence but not your hope. How to keep hoping, when hope is your only joy. How to laugh for ever.

This is the story of four mothers and their daughters – Chinese-American women, the mothers born in China, and the daughters born in America. Through their eyes we see life in pre-Revolutionary China, and life in downtown San Francisco; women struggling to find a cultural identity that can include a past and a future half a world apart.